With Our
Compliments

Curzon Interim Management Ltd
1 Heddon Street London W1B 4BD 0207 470 7167
www.curzoninterim.com

PERFECT M&As

The Art of Business Integration

Paul J. Siegenthaler

Perfect M&As
The Art of Business Integration

First published in 2009 by

Ecademy Press
6, Woodland Rise, Penryn, Cornwall, UK. TR10 8QD
info@ecademy-press.com
www.ecademy-press.com

Printed and Bound by Lightning Source in the UK and USA

Set in Zapf Elliptical 711 10pt by Charlotte Mouncey

Printed on acid-free paper from managed forests. This book is printed
on demand, so no copies will be remaindered or pulped.

ISBN 978-1-905823-63-5

Contents

Appendix   **207**

Acknowledgements

The material I have pulled together in this book is the fruit of years of experience, repeated exposure to the intensity and pace of business integrations, and lessons learnt the hard way along that journey.

I am indebted to those individuals whose inspiring leadership, detailed feedback, support, friendship and trust in my abilities have provided me with the opportunity to drive such a diverse range of international or otherwise large-scale programmes of radical business change, to learn and further develop my own skills, to experiment diverse ways of leading change, and to observe keenly the dynamics that come into play when two or more organisations blend to create something new.

My thanks to Mike Arrowsmith, Professor Christopher Bones, Walter Caldwell, Barbara Carlini, Paul Clinton, Robin Dargue, Liann Eden, Stefan Ewald, Finn Johnsson, John Jones, Jack Keenan, Tom Koza, Jeff Long, Dena McCallum, Ian Meakins, Ivan Menezes, Paul Moss, John Philips, Andy Robertson, Ian Robinson, John Stewart, Lucy Stragapede, Laurence Tanty, Peter Ward, Sharon Wayne, Edith Weber, Sharon Werner, Lindsay Wittenberg, and to all the people who worked in my teams these past 15 years across Europe and North America, demonstrating such passion, commitment and a shared common purpose. Thank you all for your guidance, your feedback and your support.

I also wish to express my gratitude to my wife Monique, who gracefully accepted that the scarce and precious free time we can spend together be further curtailed by the months it has taken me to draft my thoughts here, and to my son Nicolas who said to me: "You don't read that many books, what makes you suddenly want to *write* one?". At that moment

I realised how passionate I am about the topic of this book, and how keen I am to share the simple but numerous things that can make or break a successful business integration.

Last but not least, my thanks to Mindy Gibbins-Klein, who actually sat me down to write this book and put to paper all the things I wish I had known 15 years ago when I started tackling serious business transformation programmes.

Introduction

Place two egg yolks in a bowl; add oil; let them rest for a while. Observe… you were hoping for mayonnaise, but nothing happens. Is that at all surprising?

Likewise when bringing two companies together and expecting them to blend into a single seamless entity. Good cooks will tell you that making a perfect mayonnaise is an art. Executives managing a merger or major acquisition often view the integration exercise as a mere process that needs to be executed. They believe that the pieces of the puzzle will automatically fall into place after some time. And yet there is clear evidence that this is not the case. Just as a mayonnaise can curdle, so can organisations. When that happens, putting things right again can be incredibly difficult; in some instances the damage will be irreversible.

Estimates of the proportion of mergers and acquisitions that fail vary widely, possibly because there are different interpretations of what constitutes a failure. Wharton accounting professor Robert Holthausen states that most published research on this topic situates the failure rate between 50% and 80%. A survey by KPMG International places the threshold at the 80% top end.

> *Every company embarking on an acquisition or merger assumes it will succeed, when in fact it should assume it will fail unless it engages in a number of specific activities and avoids the many traps into which all the failed mergers have fallen, time and time again.*

I prefer to focus on success and think of the 20% of companies that actually succeed in reaching the goals they had set themselves in merging or making an important acquisition, and understand what it takes to be sure of being one of those few success stories. But even so, this is an alarmingly low proportion. Every company embarking on an organisational merger assumes it will succeed, when in fact it should assume it will fail unless it engages in a number of specific activities and avoids the many traps into which all the failed mergers have fallen, time and time again.

At a high level, the definition of 'success' is the creation of value for the company, which itself is derived either from improved earnings, or some form of strategic advantage that improves the company's prospects compared to its pre-merger position. My own definition of a successful integration goes one step further, to include not only the final outcome, but the way one got there. I would mark an integration with a 'pass' if the business case underlying the merger or acquisition is delivered; in other words if the integration project is completed on time, within budget (the costs as well as the savings), and results in an organisation that surpasses what the two constituent parts could have achieved individually in terms of Return on Investment and Growth Rate. And I would give the score of 'pass with distinction' if, in addition to delivering the business case, the integration can have taken place in an orderly manner that has retained knowledge and key staff, has provided a number of people in the organisation with an opportunity for self-development, and more broadly has given the organisation a level of comfort in executing the integration that generates an appetite for future similar acquisitions and a continued acceleration of their growth.

There is evidence to show that companies that make regular acquisitions and make this one of their core competencies tend to perform better than their peers[1]. This is the good news, because it does mean that not all is random when it comes to the art of integrating companies: there are some lessons that can be learnt and applied.

---

[1] Prof. Martin Sikora, Editor of Mergers & Acquisitions: The Dealmaker's Journal

Not all is random when it comes to the art of integrating companies: there are some lessons that can be learnt and applied.

And yet, looking across the market at the broad diversity of companies that attempt to merge or integrate an acquisition, it seems that the same mistakes are made repeatedly. The consulting firms that provide advice and support to their clients throughout their integration have a wealth of experience; they have done this dozens or hundreds of times before. Yet the brutal truth is that only 20% of these integration journeys reach the objective they had set themselves, while the majority will miss it, and a significant portion of them will actually destroy value. I find this most frustrating, for while it is true that there are myriad things to bear in mind when integrating two companies, it is not rocket science.

The knowledge and experience accumulated by reputed consulting firms often fails to influence their clients' senior leadership when they are about to set out on an integration journey. This is because they tend to dismiss the long 'to do' list provided by their consulting advisors; they may view this as over-kill and probably suspect it is a ploy for the consultants to gain even more business by involving as many resources as possible in the integration project. In the haste and flurry of activity that precedes the announcement of a merger or major acquisition, they do not have the time nor the appetite to not only absorb the long list of things that are important to achieve a successful integration, but to actually consider and truly grasp *why* these things are important.

Having designed and led company integrations involving up to 12 countries, and managed these not as a consultant but on the client's 'side', I decided to write this book to share my observations of what really makes the difference between success and failure from the moment the merger or acquisition deal is about to be signed until the two organisations have blended into one and reached stability.

So much goes on during the integration of two organisations, particularly when these cover a large geographical spread, that it is easy to lose sight of the overall process and omit a few fairly simple things. Most of the literature on mergers and acquisitions states that the causes of failed integrations are a lack of communication, weak leadership and poor handling of aspects relating to human resources. Although this is almost certainly the case, such a broad statement hardly provides any clues as to what needs to be done to ensure success, and how this should be delivered.

I therefore chose to go one step further and put my finger on the specific things that make a big difference. This book digs deeper to observe and understand the consequences of specific behaviours, as well as the impact of the way the integration project is organised and run. It explains why some people will surpass themselves during inordinately stressful times and remain committed to the objective of the integration.

I felt it important to share these insights with any executive who is about to lead a company integration, as well as with the numerous managers who will be expected to play a role in its successful outcome.

I have tried to keep the book as short as possible while nonetheless covering all the aspects that need to be considered. This is aimed at allowing the reader to grasp the entire content from cover to cover, and then refer back to specific chapters as the integration progresses through its various stages to ensure the various tips and recommendations made here are being applied, and to check the 'temperature' of the organisation along the way.

The objective is clear: it is to be among those 20% of companies that can claim, when all is over, that their decision to merge was the right one, that it was executed brilliantly, and that by doing so they have generated significant value.

> *The objective is clear: it is to be among those 20% of companies that can claim, when all is over, that their decision to merge was the right one, that it was executed brilliantly, and that by doing so they have generated significant value.*

Strategic Intent of the Merger or Acquisition

Objectives and scope

Who sets them

Quite unsurprisingly, different people have different expectations from one same project, and the integration of two companies is no exception. However, the very notion of 'integrating' two organisations implies an intention to obtain alignment and common focus, and consequently the very first mistake many companies make takes place right at the onset of the voyage they have decided to embark upon together, by failing to paint a clear and coherent picture of their shared vision, values and aims. And therefore it is quite normal that the mental energy of most of the individuals in both organisations will be wasted on hypothesising whether theirs is a merger of equals, or a take-over, a convergence towards 'best of both', the overthrow of one company's culture by the other's, or a common journey towards totally new ways of working.

In a perfect world, one would hope that the reasons for a merger or acquisition should be so abundantly clear that they would not require much explanation. Sadly, such blatantly obvious opportunities are not that frequent, and Boards of Directors need to go to great efforts and lengthy, often convoluted, explanations to convince their shareholders of the cogency of their merger or acquisition proposal. Considering that many sources estimate that almost 50% of mergers end up destroying shareholder value, it is quite amazing in this day and age that so many shareholders give their vote of confidence to a Board that asks them to approve a major decision which they struggle to justify and is likely to result in failure. Or will the Board apply the lessons learnt from the many failed company integrations and maintain theirs on a course towards success, value creation, and the acceleration of future growth?

Hostile take-overs possibly present the advantage of providing some clarity from the onset about who sets the rules – although the challenges appear later on when the organisation that was 'conquered' is required to integrate seamlessly into the new enlarged company.

On the other hand, while most 'friendly' acquisitions and mergers attempt to present a single face to the outside world as early as possible, many of them try to display a sense of balance and consensus internally by placing two individuals in each of the key roles at the top of the organisation. This was the case, for example, during the merger of Guinness Plc and Grand Metropolitan Plc, which decided to unite their destiny and become the world's leading premium spirits company, Diageo Plc. From the day the decision to merge was made public, until the day some seven months later when the merger of the industry's number one and number two was approved by the European and North American regulatory authorities, the CEOs of the two divisions that were destined to be integrated, toured the world in a major road show as CEO and Deputy CEO of the future organisation.

This was intended to illustrate to the employees of both companies that this was a 'merger of equals', with both the CEO and his Deputy broadcasting the same carefully crafted messages across the entire organisation. However, no company can durably have two individuals in the top seat: while the well-rehearsed duo were performing their World Roadshow, the bets were on as to which of the two would ultimately leave the company. This then paved the way for speculation as to which of the two companies would have the top hand in shaping the future merged organisation.

> *It is amazing that so many shareholders give their vote of confidence to a Board by approving a merger or major acquisition which they struggle to justify and is likely to result in failure*

In complex organisations, once the investor community has been convinced of the validity of the integration's business case, the CEO's key role will be to ensure that everyone throughout the organisation understands the vision and is prepared to make the efforts necessary to reach that visionary goal. Much of *how* this will be achieved will, in many cases, be delegated to the next echelon of the company's management, who will be left with the arduous task of defining the exact scope of the integration voyage. As in any major project, the person or body that will make those decisions must have the acknowledged authority to do so, to ensure that all of the people and departments impacted by the project are considered. In many instances, the Finance function is given the lead of the integration's implementation process, although it is also frequent to see some naturally project-oriented functions such as IT or Manufacturing volunteering to take that lead. The key point I want to make here is that regardless of who ends up leading the integration programme, it must be based on solid governance that will ensure that all decisions contribute towards the realisation of the merger's or acquisition's vision and business case.

The other pre-requisite when choosing the 'champion' of the integration is to ensure that this individual will remain in the company throughout the integration process, which can last anywhere between six months in simple organisations to two or three years in large multi-nationals. If the integration lasts over three years, chances are it is being badly managed!

Setting the *right* objectives

Even when the right people have been selected to set the objectives and scope of a merger or integration, it is only too easy to yield to the temptation of throwing in some 'nice to have' add-ons. Wanting to become 'world class' in a number of areas is partly the result of egos of the CEO and members of the Executive team, and is also partly due to the belief that the newly enlarged size of the integrated organisation makes the pursuit of world class affordable. The less glitzy reality of business life is that all that matters is to be better than your competitors in areas where this differentiation will provide you with a decisive competitive advantage. This need not necessarily be 'world class', and certainly does not apply to all aspects of a business. In spite of that, we have all heard or read about these companies that, at the onset of their integration, define this milestone as the beginning of a new golden age of perfection. The concept of perfection is attractive, of course, but the quest for world-class standards in areas that will not provide the integrated organisation with a decisive competitive advantage is likely to detract focus and energy from laying the basic foundation of the new company, where it is most needed.

Integrating companies while continuing to drive day-to-day business is an exhausting exercise that will be carried out by resources which, by definition, are limited. Focus and ruthless prioritisation are key, and therefore being very selective when setting the scope is a necessary discipline. Ask yourself when refining the scope of your integration programme: "Do we *really* need this to deliver the business case?" and "*how soon* do we need it?".

Scope creep

Scope creep is one of the gravest dangers along the path of an integration programme. New opportunities arise as time goes by. Some of these will arise from new events on the market or changes in the company's environment. Cross-functional teams might identify others as they get a better overall understanding of the business. It is difficult not to include the latter into the scope of the original programme, because they are perceived as something that was overlooked and should have been included into the initial scope.

Regardless of whether the opportunity is internal or exogenous to the organisation, you need to recognise that unless you re-prioritise the initiatives that form part of the programme, one of the key variables of the programme will change: longer time, or more resources - both of which mean more costs or alternatively deliberately reducing quality or abandoning another initiative in the current plans. Always ask yourself "Do we need this now, or can it wait?" and also, importantly, "Can we manage any more activity than we already are?". If the organisation is fortunate enough to be able to absorb the additional activity required to deliver the new initiative, it may be worthwhile considering that initiative as a separate project rather than adding it to the scope of the integration programme, primarily to avoid the loss of momentum that affects major programmes that are seen to extend indefinitely and just drag on and on.

Therefore be prepared to seriously challenge every aspect of the programme's scope – obviously at the onset before the integration begins, but also during formal reviews as with time there might be opportunities to *reduce* or tighten the scope, allowing you to complete the integration faster and/or at less cost. Always keep in mind that every deliverable of the integration programme must be 'fit for purpose', which in the large majority of cases will not necessarily mean 'world class'.

Setting the initial goal:
One face to the customer

Ask three people in the same organisation how long their integration process lasted and you will almost certainly obtain three different answers. Whereas the starting point of the integration is clearly identified, its end point is not. Large international organisations may take a number of years to fully integrate their information systems and re-shape their manufacturing footprint, and until this is done one cannot say that the two companies are seamlessly integrated throughout their entire structure. While this prolonged transition state does not necessarily make them vulnerable on the market, any opportunity left open to customers or suppliers to play one part of the merging company against the other is likely to be exploited and *will* destroy value.

Therefore what really matters is to present **one face to the customer**, and that crucial milestone is characterised by the following:

- One trading name replaces the former two companies' names.

- Harmonised trading terms and conditions.

- Integrated portfolio of products and/or services.

- Integrated sales force.

- Integrated customer service.

- Customers can buy a combination of products or services or the two former companies in a single order, and pay for these to one same bank account.

At this stage, some merged companies will still need to raise two invoices for a single order placed by customers and possibly make two deliveries because their supply chain has not yet been merged and the IT systems are linked to the supply chain. The format and layout of the two invoices might differ, but they are both raised in the name of one single company. This clearly is not optimal from the customers' perspective, but what really matters is that the commercial proposition presented to the customers is unified and coherent and these customers cannot try to 'divide and conquer' by cherry-picking the most favourable terms and prices offered by the two former companies.

By the time they are ready to present 'one face to the customer', many merging organisations can more generally present 'one face to the outside world', thereby also presenting a united interface towards their suppliers. This can contribute significant value if the combined size of the merged organisation gives the company the added clout that enables it to re-negotiate future supply contracts beyond the advantages that would naturally result from the larger consolidated purchase quantities.

Other key milestones of an integration may take far longer, and this can be for a number of reasons ranging from employee consultation procedures, which can greatly extend the duration of the process in some countries, to intricate technicalities and regulations, as would be the case when merging the pension funds of two business entities, rolling out a new integrated IT platform, or re-shaping the manufacturing footprint.

It follows that the initial focus of the integration must be to present 'one face to the customer'. Until that is achieved, the merging business remains exposed, and common sense tells us that this state of vulnerability must come to an end as soon as practically possible.

Speed matters

Timing is critical during integration projects, not only in terms of synchronising the pace of numerous activities to ensure their milestones coincide, but also to maintain momentum: speed matters. The longer the integration process drags on, the more it is likely to cost the company, not only in terms of direct costs such as consultant support, temporary contractors and delays in realising the cost synergies, but also in terms of lost revenue because the individuals in both organisations are likely to tire out and miss sales or business development opportunities.

You need to maintain pace to give a sense of urgency, boost energy levels and prevent in every possible way the people in the organisation from getting the impression that their voyage towards integration is just a painful never-ending story.

Drawing on his rich experience at the helm of internationally renowned corporations, Jack Keenan[2], told a gathering of senior managers from two companies that were about to embark on a worldwide merger: *"Merging organisations is like pulling out teeth: you can do it slow and painful, or quick and painful. We shall do it quick and painful"*.

So how long should it take, you might ask. The answer depends obviously on how dissimilar the two organisations are today compared

---

[2] Jack Keenan, former Chairman Kraft Foods International, Deputy CEO United Distillers & Vintners, Executive Director Diageo Plc, Non-Exec Director The Body Shop International Plc and Marks & Spencer Plc.

to the desired end-state and on the number of barriers and obstacles that might hinder the pace of progression. If the journey lasts more than a year until the business can present 'one face to the customer', it is likely that a number of people in the organisation will lose patience or get discouraged, and you may lose some of your key players as a result of attrition. As always in such circumstances, the people who will jump ship are not those you can dispense with, nor are they the people you felt would anyway drop out at some stage as a result of the integration of the two organisations. Of course not. The first people to leave are those who have found a good position somewhere else, because their skills and competencies – as well as maybe the experience they have acquired in your company – make them excellent candidates on the job market. And you are thus losing some of your best elements and over time their departure will give out a strong negative signal throughout the company. Those of their colleagues who feel they have the necessary credentials to do likewise may be tempted to jump ship too, or at the very least will lose focus and energy by spending their time thinking about it or 'testing the market', and the rest of the organisation - those who feel they are less attractive on the job market - will begin to get seriously worried and de-motivated.

I have experienced three ways in which one can prevent this attrition phenomenon from occurring:

- Regardless of the overall duration of the integration process, always make sure that throughout the organisation people feel that things are moving as fast as possible. Beyond having a well-organised integration programme to ensure you can actually achieve that speed, you will want people to know about it. Hence the importance of communication, and that is communication in the broad sense, which also includes body language and behaviours, which I shall come back to later (see Chapter 9).

- The second important way in which the overall duration of the integration can be made to *feel* shorter is preparation: all the analysis, planning, preparation and activities that can take place *before* the kick-off of the integration process, or in many cases before the merger or acquisition deal is even completed. This is very often overlooked and is yet so important. Thorough, intelligent and well-organised pre-integration preparation can make the difference between a brilliantly executed integration and a long-drawn flop. I am passionate about this because I have seen the benefits of it in real-life situations, and conversely the sometimes deplorable results of poor preparation. This is why I have dedicated a whole section of the book to this topic (see Chapter 5).

▪ Thirdly, breaking the overall integration programme into a series of key stages will avert feelings among the staff that the company has embarked on a never-ending saga. This allows everyone to focus on one chapter at a time, starting with the initial thrust to achieve 'one face to the customer', which can then be followed by the integration of the IT platform, full integration of the supply chain, the re-shaping of the manufacturing footprint, pension fund integration etc.

Value versus egos and personal agendas

Megalomania and other big ideas

Publicly quoted companies would do well to trust the commonsense of their shareholders. If the business case in favour of a merger or major acquisition is very difficult to sell to the investor community, why do some people believe it will be easier to sell to the stakeholders *within* the company and to those people who will be impacted by the proposed changes? When the benefits case of a merger is not blatantly obvious, why would people deliberately want to engage on the rocky and treacherous path of a major company integration? Many merger proposals are motivated by the desire to become the biggest in the industry. In economic terms size matters, being 'big enough' is important, but this does not mean that bigger is automatically better because size is also a factor of complexity and can potentially lead to lack of focus. But regardless of the cogency of the merger proposition, the team at the top of the organisation will have their moment of glory in the media and be the talk of the town.

There is, to my knowledge, no systematic research on this topic, but somehow I strongly suspect that many mergers, and indeed some of the mega-mergers such as those that have occurred in the past ten to fifteen years, are motivated at least as much by the ego of the people at the helm of those organisations as by any rational economic value-adding proposition. It is not hard to imagine how proud an individual would feel by creating overnight the largest company of its industry. Such a venture fulfils the quest for power and domination that is buried deep in the subconscious of many humans, certainly among many of the males of the species. The prospect of significant personal wealth is another factor, but then wealth is nothing more than another vector of power.

No person in their right mind would be willing to admit in public that the main reason for the merger or acquisition they recommend is to provide them with a fantastic ego trip, and so some form of post-rationalised benefit needs to be thought of, in the hope of convincing the shareholders of the soundness of the proposed plan. If that proposal is sufficiently convincing to sway the shareholders towards a positive vote, it had better be compelling enough to also achieve acceptance and buy-in from the organisations' employees, or else the integration journey will be a tortuous one. Let's remember Jack Keenan's comparison of mergers and pulling teeth: nobody wants to opt for the "slow and painful" approach if at all avoidable!

Ruthless focus on a good benefits case

The better and more convincingly a benefits case can be articulated, the easier the integration will be, because everyone involved will have clarity as to the end purpose of the efforts they will be required to make during the transition period. And while in almost every case the benefits of a merger or major acquisition will be economic profit, it is worth remembering that many of the drivers of economic value can also be quite palatable to employees, consumers, local communities or the tax authorities. This is the case for example when the future combined structure will enable accelerated growth, increased investment in new product development, or more clout in promoting certain social values associated with a particular company or trademark.

Getting shareholder approval for a merger is the first hurdle to overcome, and so in too many instances the benefits case focuses solely on the value creation that the merger promises to deliver to the company's investors. However, it makes sense to also consider the integration efforts that will follow beyond the actual merger or acquisition *transaction*. Think beyond the immediate value creation for the shareholders and give some thorough consideration to the benefits the combination of the two companies might provide to other stakeholder groups. These will form the basis for your communication platform throughout the integration process. There will be hurdles to overcome, nerves will become frayed, some people will begin to wonder why the company ever embarked on this difficult voyage. You will need to repeat the 'reason why' consistently during the whole integration process to maintain a sense of common purpose and direction within the two companies as they blend gradually with one another.

Justifying the choice that was made

Read the trade press or in-house company communications: too often, company mergers or major acquisitions are presented almost as a *fait accompli*, the only possible choice. And yet, the benefits proposition could appear that much stronger if one had taken the time to explain what the alternatives were and why the proposed way forward chosen. In what way it is better than all the possible alternatives? You can generate real 'buy-in' by showing how much better the strategy is compared to those alternatives, because for most of the members of staff and management, knowing they are working for a smart organisation which is one cut above the rest will be a strong source of pride, satisfaction and identity.

Our intellectualised approach of business makes us shy away from 'obvious' solutions – there is nothing very remarkable about embarking on an 'obvious' path. And yet, what you want the people in your organisation to think throughout the integration process is: "of course we should be doing this". But to achieve that "of course", the reason why must be obvious, self-explanatory. This does not prevent your project from being ambitious and bold, maybe even a little scary to some. Nonetheless, remember that every individual who is acquired to the idea that "of course we need to do this", will be a self-fuelled proactive player and valuable catalyst for change throughout the integration journey.

In Essence...

- *Be very selective when setting the scope. Do we really need this to deliver the business case, how soon do we need it.*

- *Review / challenge priorities: do we need this now, or can it wait?*

- *Fit for purpose does not mean world class.*

- *Minimise vulnerability: achieve one face to the customer as soon as possible.*

- *Speed matters: maintain momentum. Give a sense of speed: communicate progress, good preparation accelerates implementation, break the long journey into stages.*

- *Is the benefits case compelling for all key stakeholders; what were the alternatives? Repeat it often so everyone knows why they are doing this.*

The So-called 'Soft Aspects'

Giving some meaning to 'Change Management'

What others say

Most of the literature and theories covering Change Management might be useful in understanding some of the root causes of human behaviour in situations of change – albeit very often in a rather over-intellectualised way – but are hardly helpful when it comes to doing anything to redirect those behaviours towards a desired outcome. It is no wonder that Change Management remains an obscure science for the layman when some writers mention they draw their tools from schools of thought such as 'Theme Centred Interaction', 'Gestalt Therapy', 'Neurolinguistic Programming', 'Chaos Theory' or 'Quantum Physics'.

Personally, I find it easier to understand what is, after all, a fairly general and quite universal observation of human behaviour and putting myself in someone else's shoes rather than trying to plot individuals onto specific phases of a 'change curve' as they struggle their way through denial, despondency, acceptance, buy-in and commitment. When it comes to leading people through change, in my opinion it is more valuable to learn how to decrypt people's behaviours, understand what they are *really* trying to say, and *pull* them through the journey of change rather than pushing them down that path. Decrypting those messages can become very complex when you are dealing with business integrations that span several countries and cultures. Just as spoken language is different, so is the unspoken communication – and those differences are all the more treacherous that there is no official dictionary to decode body language and behaviours. You may be in for some bad surprises if you *expect* those signals to be similar just because the spoken language and culture are similar or identical. I have been caught out more than once in assuming that Germans would react like Austrians, or that Americans in New England would react in a way that would be very similar to their colleagues in 'Olde England'. Beware!

Cross-cultural awareness is therefore a must. Nonetheless, the good news is that there are – thankfully – a few common traits that will apply almost invariably across all business cultures.

Fear of change: routine save us

What is so difficult or complicated about initiating and managing change? Just think of a few scenarios, simple things you may have observed around you daily. A cat crossing a garden every day, walking along exactly the same path. The way regular commuters tend to wait for their train on the platform at the same spot every day, because they know that is where the door of the wagon will be, and that their wagon is the one that gives them the shortest walk when they get off to either exit their station or catch a connecting train. Or maybe the list of things you do first thing in the morning when you get out of bed. Or the sequence in which you put on your clothes. Or the way we drive to work and get there not remembering much about the trip, as though we were on auto-pilot, day after day. Biologically, the human being has not evolved that much in the past 3,000 years and yet the accepted wisdom of our century is that routine is dull, that it makes life boring and is not 'cool'.

Quite to the contrary, if you think of it, routine is in fact what prevents us from collapsing with mental overload before the morning is over. Routine saves us as a biological species, because anything we do as a routine is a proven and safe way of getting things done. Anything we can do as a routine leaves us with some spare mental bandwidth to cope with exceptional items and be on the lookout for anything dangerous or threatening in our immediate environment.

Fear saves us too. Fear is one of the essential mechanisms thanks to which species can survive. If we didn't have that little alarm bell within each of us that rings to say 'be careful', we would all be engaging in dangerous activities that would get us into bad trouble or even get us killed. If there ever was on this planet any form of developed animal that had no sense of fear, you can be sure it is extinct today.

What I aim to illustrate here is that we would not exist today if biologically we were not somehow programmed to seek proven routines and fear the unknown. In a stable environment (and I insist on the word 'stable'), the safest and most successful key to survival is to do the same proven things over and over again, and not to venture too far into the unknown. But change that environment and things could look very different, as the dinosaurs discovered – far too late.

Importantly, when considering the magnitude of the change that will take place in your business as a result of integration, bear in mind that the resistance to change you are inevitably about to encounter is not caused by laziness or uncooperative attitudes from the people around you. That resistance finds its root cause in something much more fundamental, which lies deep within each of us: our instinctive need for safe proven routines and our apprehension of the unknown. In our society today, people will usually find it difficult to admit they are scared of forthcoming changes – some may indeed think that this could be a career limiting statement, or make them feel less able than their peers. This causes a huge risk, the risk of not recognising the early symptoms of one of the key causes of resistance to change: fear. Chances are that the vast majority of the people in your organisation have never gone through a merger or business integration before. This is a journey into the unknown, and they are aware from numerous examples that hit the headlines in the media that things can often go drastically wrong.

Some people with the best intentions might declare themselves fully on-board with a proposed change programme and still be extremely unsettled deep down inside. And if this is the case, it will not take much during the implementation of the change for such people to become sceptical and adopt a behaviour that is detrimental to the desired outcome.

As human beings, we are programmed to seek stability, safety, some form of comfort. Not to deliberately seek change, unless the need for change is made abundantly clear because above all, like all other species, we are programmed to survive. Translate this into a business environment and it is easy to understand how individuals will accept the pain and effort of change if they can be convinced that life overall will be better afterwards than where they stand today. Hence the importance of articulating the strategic intent, the "Why are we doing this?" with great clarity, as discussed earlier, as well as addressing the specific benefit to the individual, the so-called "What's in it for me?".

Big ideas take time to percolate through organisations

Individuals need *time* to absorb change. They need that time to adapt to the idea of what is expected from them, to visualise how things will feel in the future, understand how they will fit in that future, and accept to work their way proactively towards that future vision. How much time? I think the answer to that question is "more time than you would consider reasonable". Be prepared to reach the outer limits of your patience. And the reason for this is not that people lack the intelligence required to change or that they are irreparably stuck in their current paradigm, but merely that whatever you have communicated to them is totally new. You, on the other hand, have been working on the merger or acquisition strategy and so have been engrossed in it for some time and in your mind you are almost there, having completed the journey mentally. Now, the people who need to make this happen, maybe hundreds, thousands or tens of thousands of people, are required to catch up with your thinking. Give them some time to achieve this, or you will risk giving them the impression they have been forced into this against their will and against their better judgement.

There are of course a few helpful accelerators that you will need, because once an acquisition proposition is on the table, your investors will be impatient to see the benefits you have promised them. As I mentioned earlier, speed matters. And therefore waiting for the need for change to sink into people's minds is frustrating and goes against the core principle of maximising the speed of integration. This will clearly sound incredibly trivial, but the first logical step is to avoid anything that may slow down the acceptance of change. And yet all too often one can observe during company integrations that the rejection of change has resulted from senior management's attempts to 'cut corners' and move ahead faster than the troops could cope with. Why would senior managers be so unperceptive you might ask?

One of the key reasons for this is that, in line with the notion that 'time matters', staff briefings tend to be given in rather large groups for the sake of efficiency and because information needs to percolate rapidly through the strata of the organisation. The further down you go, the larger the numbers, the further the individuals are removed from the strategic orientation and vision of the company – and therefore the more effort one may need to put in to obtain their buy-in to the vision and objectives of the proposed integration. The very words 'merger', 'acquisition' or 'integration' will flash alarm signals in many people's minds because they are synonymous with upheaval and possibly redundancy. In such situations, people will either try to shine and come across as *the* individuals the future organisation must absolutely retain or will otherwise (in much greater numbers) adopt a very low profile.

Put yourself in that frame of mind and imagine you are among a crowd with 20, 50 or one hundred of your colleagues, and you will understand why people do *not* ask questions after briefings, even if ten questions are burning their tongue. They are most unlikely to openly disclose their concerns or fear, either verbally or in their body language, because this would be an admission of vulnerability in a world in which we are told to be bold high performers.

Consequently it is not a surprise that so many managers, at the end of a briefing during which they informed their staff of developments that may have far reaching consequences for them, feel afterwards that "all went well" and that "no difficult questions were asked". In large circles in the presence of senior managers and numerous colleagues it is unlikely anyone will ask questions, even if you have asked some of your close lieutenants to prepare some questions in advance of the briefing to kick-off a debate. All too often these initial questions are followed by a somewhat embarrassing silence, after which all you can do is thank the audience for their attention and let them know you remain available to answer the questions they might have in the coming days.

The most commonly used method of capturing at least some feedback after such briefings is to organise small workshops in the following days, in groups of 10 to 20 people, to discuss in a smaller circle the implications of the recent announcements. This facilitation of dialogue encourages individuals to voice their thoughts and concerns, and can work well in some cultures and completely miss the point in another. Asking people to challenge ideas in group discussions is a particularly Anglo-Saxon concept. I have also observed this working well in French companies, as the confrontation of ideas and contradictory debates tend to be at the heart of French culture, but this can occasionally be hampered by the presence of a very charismatic or directive manager who cramps the participants' willingness to express and share their thoughts and feelings. It would be a little hazardous to draw sweeping generalisations but nonetheless most people's experience of such situations in a Germanic environment will find that it will take longer and require more effort to generate and facilitate the dialogue because the German business culture in most companies is less suited to cathartic group discussions. Therefore it may take a while to get a proper understanding of the individuals' concerns and ensure one has adequately responded to those concerns.

I have on several occasions given briefings to staff in Austria and Germany announcing bleak restructuring measures of their company. As usual, such briefings kick off with an explanation of the company's vision, the pressures of its environment and competition, the need to remain ahead of competition. At that point, things become a little more difficult: some individuals will be winners and will benefit from the forthcoming changes, others will be clear losers and are likely to lose their job. A Human Resources manager of a company in which I worked back in 1994 was dispatched from London headquarters to Austria to be by my side during one such delicate briefing. Almost one third of the people present were going to have to face redundancy. At the end of my briefing, the audience applauded. One individual, who knew he was likely to be one of the casualties of the company's restructuring, stated that this was a very bold and courageous plan and the right thing for the company to do. The very puzzled HR manager then asked me whether they had understood what I had told them! Of course they had, as they were being briefed in their own language. The point here is that none of them felt it appropriate to open the debate or ask questions relating to personal concerns in the presence of their colleagues.

The above real story might be a little extreme, but let us not fall into the trap of clichés and believe that the reaction would have been totally different in markets other than Germany or Austria. Giving important briefings to large audiences can be useful to give the news a feeling of importance and make it eventful. It is also economical in the sense that very senior management can be involved in a limited number of events. Everyone will be aware that this is not about business as usual, and that something will change. What that something really is remains to be clarified and understood, and that clarification must occur very soon afterwards, before everyone has had time to guess a scenario that would almost certainly be wrong.

Always remember that at first, most people will not volunteer to ask questions. Do not assume they are OK. Peer pressure is strong; people will say "yes" to look brave, but deep down inside, they mean "no". To convince yourself of this, try this very simple test – it is easy and fun, and I have done it a number of times and it never fails. Ask a large audience of one hundred of more people whether they agree that most people are afraid of change and are likely to resist it. Let us bet that at least three quarters of the audience will raise their hand. Now ask that same audience who in the room is personally afraid of change and likely to resist it – you will inevitably hear embarrassed laughter, and if more than half a dozen hands raise, others may follow and you can consider yourself lucky to be standing in front of an audience of incredibly open-minded and candid people who have great trust in each other. So far I have never had that luck. My last two 'tests' in front of 150 and 180 people respectively resulted in a show of zero hands, but nonetheless a lot of embarrassed laughter in the room! The anecdote may sound amusing, but behind it lies an important observation: most people have a somewhat 'macho' side to them when placed in a competitive business environment, which prevents them from admitting vulnerability, fear, or lack of understanding.

It will usually require a series of discussions in very small groups, or possibly even numerous one-on-one meetings, to ensure you have a correct perception of where everyone stands and what obstacles remain to achieve acceptance and, subsequently, buy-in. In a large group, individuals may think "my question is a little silly and doesn't interest the others". In a very small group of similar and possibly like-minded colleagues, their questions might actually be helpful for their colleagues, and the degree of familiarity between the people in the group will allow each one to venture out with some more personal questions. If possible, make sure a repeat of those gatherings is organised a few days later, once the attendees have had time to digest the information and match it to their own individual circumstances and needs – this will generate further questions and bring more clarity. Reducing that fear of the unknown is the first step towards allowing individuals to contemplate the facts, understand what is required from them and what is in it for them, without being blinded by feelings of panic deep down inside.

I think it is fair to say that most companies underestimate the time that is needed to percolate big messages through an organisation, unless they have a very clear communication plan from the out-set with realistic timelines and a simple compelling message. That communication plan will need to consider how many small group briefings can be set up to deliver a clear message to the relevant target audiences while still achieving this within a reasonable time-span; there is a fine balance to be achieved here between the speed and quality of the delivery. I mentioned earlier that speed matters when it comes to integrating businesses, but speed here means pace, rather than race.

> *People will say "yes" to look brave, but deep down inside, they mean "no"*

It's okay to say "I don't know"

In today's business culture, people are led to believe they must know the answers to every possible question they may face. This must be a remnant from our school days – getting good marks for answering the greatest number of questions thrown at the classroom by the teacher. Following that same pattern, many managers preparing business reviews spend at least as much time preparing back-up slides and information packs as they do for the core presentation or document, in order to be prepared for every single eventuality. Some company cultures may actually require and expect this, and it is not my intention here to discuss whether this is a good or bad thing. The reality is that when two organisations announce their intention to integrate, you can be prepared for most of the generic questions that are likely to emerge, but it is unlikely you will have the background information required to correctly answer some personal questions once people start digging into the detail.

And yet, when briefings are given regarding most forms of profound business change, many managers appear to feel that they *must* be in a position to give an answer to every question to avoid looking weak, careless or out of control. This will incite them to guess what the answer should be, or express what they would like that answer to be, or voice what they think the audience would like to hear. Do not get caught in that trap! Unlike the hands raised in the classroom where with a little luck an inspired guess can turn out to be the right answer, when it comes to business and more particularly to the future of individuals facing a company integration, not giving an answer is by far preferable to giving the wrong answer, because you will be held accountable for your wrong answer and this could have very nasty consequences.

It is alright to say "I don't know". As long as the overall message and strategic intent are well articulated and make sense, and that people get a feel for the what lies ahead, most individuals will be receptive to the fact that senior management have decided to carry out the integration in a well thought-through manner and will not be rushed into decisions that affect the daily lives and careers of their people. I have observed in many situations that saying "I don't know actually" *reinforces* an individual's credibility, because it is an expression of honesty, a sign of transparent and open communication, a demonstration that the manager giving the briefing is not making up the story as he or she speaks.

There is, however, an important imperative add-on to the phrase "I don't know", which is to let the audience know that the question has been noted and will be followed-up and that you expect to have an answer by a certain date. This will require you to be organised and methodical: if the date you had forecasted comes up and you still do not have an answer, you absolutely must get back to that same forum of people and explain what progress has been achieved to date and when they are likely to receive the answer you had promised. This can be a little tedious, but it pays dividends. Always make sure your staff know that their questions and concerns have been listened to, understood, and are being addressed by the relevant people within the organisation. This is the only way to prevent individuals from feeling abandoned and alienated by the integration process.

Repetition – in a balanced way

Integrating two organisations is a journey and people will experience or discover new things along the way. After the initial 'road show' of briefings and workshops destined to spread the message and rally the troops to the cause of the forthcoming integration, a large number of people across the whole company will be working feverishly on the implementation of that integration. Within that flurry of activity, it may prove difficult to take a step back and allow the time required for further briefings and up-dates. And yet, as weeks go by, the impact of the initial communication will fade and its relevance may diminish because many people will have new questions on their mind as events develop.

Organising other big events to reiterate the core messages may be perceived as being somewhat 'over the top', or may even be counterproductive if the intensity of the communication leads the audiences to feel there is a lot of 'hype' and not much substance. On the other hand, without making a big fuss about things, it is well worth bolting an additional point dedicated to the integration programme onto the agenda of as many of the company's regular meetings as possible, during which the core messages of the strategic intent can be reiterated over and over again. These short sessions have the advantage of placing the integration within the context of day-to-day business, which allows the participants to exchange thoughts, raise issues and resolve problems that feel tangible, and thus keeps them focused rather than letting them worry about the uncertainties of the longer term future.

You will need to find the right balance when injecting reminders and reiterating the core messages, to ensure continued understanding of the integration's vision and purpose, without reaching the stage of overload - just in the same way as a balloonist needs to activate the burners at regular intervals to maintain the hot air balloon at an even altitude: too much and the gas will soon run out, too little and the balloon will drop dangerously. Do not get blinded by the volume of activity surrounding the integration; allow yourself to remain receptive, be as approachable as is practically feasible. This will help you keep your finger on the pulse and understand, almost instinctively, how much communication, discussion and coaching is required without falling into the trap of over-communication.

Change across the layers of the organisation

Gut-feel and intellect

One opportunity that is often missed when communicating about the integration of companies is getting the middle management fully on board, not only by capturing and addressing their concerns as discussed above, but by also obtaining their intellectual buy-in to the strategy underlying the integration, and improving their understanding and involvement in the way the future company will operate. As their role will require them to drive the integration in their respective business units, they need to fully understand the 'big picture', rather than just what it will mean for them and their teams.

A merger or major acquisition usually marks a leap forward in the history of a company, and the work required to integrate the two organisations requires more cross-functional work than everyday business does, because most of the processes and ways of working of the future merged organisation will need to be redefined. This is an ideal environment, possibly a once in a lifetime opportunity, for middle management to peer above the boundaries of their department and get a sound understanding of those cross-functional interdependencies, thereby obtaining a good grasp not only of *how* information and value-added flow through the organisation, but also *why* the company has decided to structure itself in that way.

Observing middle managers through this transition phase can also provide useful information relating to an individual's potential for lateral development within the organisation as well as for upwards hierarchic development, given that the need to broaden one's understanding across the functional delineations of a company increases as one progresses towards the tip of the pyramid.

Whilst most managers in large companies can 'recite' the company's vision and the outline of its strategy, I find it rather sad that in many cases they cannot really articulate that strategy and understand the expected benefits of their company's strategy over other alternatives. As the integration of two companies marks the beginning of a new era, use this opportunity to get people involved, arouse their interest, and generate a more proactive and participative behaviour, because this will be one of the best ways of promoting a sense of identification with the company's destiny and you will want as many people as possible to feel this sense of identity as this will in turn give them the resolve to achieve the goals the company has set itself. At that point, by fostering 'intellectual buy-in', you will actually have transformed behaviours and created a sense of alignment and common purpose. This is the cement you will need to maintain cohesion in the company as it progresses through the challenges and stress of integration.

Driving change at the coal face

I have kept the biggest hurdle for the end of this section: the cascade of briefings and feedback from group discussions will give you a feel for the aspects of change that will be the most challenging, and the in-depth understanding of your management will ensure that everyone is clear on what needs to be done and why. But pause a moment and reflect on who the individuals are that will be most affected by the changes the integration will cause.

Think of the people in field sales, confronted with a new product range – possibly one that they considered until lately as head-on competition and now have to sell. Think of the clerks performing order entry, having to master a new suite of software, with more products and customers than previously. Think of staff picking orders in the warehouses, struggling to familiarise themselves with a new document flow, new product codes, new dispatch procedures, new product packaging. Think of the people in the purchasing department, faced with new authorisation procedures, new supplies, loss of contact with some of their former suppliers whose contracts will be terminated for the sake of rationalisation during the integration process.

There are good reasons to worry for these people, and make sure enough thought, time and effort are devoted to helping them through the forthcoming transition phase, because generally:

a) They are managed by subject matter experts, not people managers.

b) Their efficiency results from the flawless execution of a repetitive set of tasks.

c) They are being asked to reverse learned behaviours and brand allegiance.

A. People managers versus subject matter experts

In most companies, with the exception of field sales, the majority of the people who are at the 'coal face' are often managed by one of their former peers rather than by someone well versed in people management. The best order clerks become team supervisors, likewise in managing warehouse teams. Much of the value these team leaders bring to the organisation, as well as the respect they earn from their direct reports, is derived from the fact that they are experts in almost all aspects of their direct reports' work. They can manage the induction of new staff, answer almost any question they receive from members of their team, and have the potential to become role models.

This clear and simple structure breaks down when everything begins to change in a company, and it is easy to understand how these team leaders will find themselves in the most awkward situation. Their leadership was based on knowledge, not on people management skills. Whereas middle and senior managers higher up in the organisation structure may have the leadership and people management skills required to drive their teams through periods of uncertainty or ambiguity, the leaders of teams operating 'on the front' are unlikely to know how to react when faced with the anxiety of the members of their teams while the new organisation is being designed, and their subsequent frustration as they struggle to get accustomed to new software, new products, new customers and new ways of working.

Remember that their status and authority will be threatened if they lose their role as an expert in the eyes of their teams' members. This means that in terms of being informed and kept in the picture, but also in terms of being trained on the new products, processes and ways of working, these team leaders need to be kept constantly one step ahead of the game. Team leaders tend to have accumulated more years of service in a company than their direct reports; they will also in most cases be their seniors in terms of age. Therefore they may be a little more set in their ways than the people they are meant to lead and, worse, if the changes they must implement involve new technology or software, it is possible that some of the young keen members of their teams will grasp this much faster than they will. Most team leaders will find this prospect very unsettling. They will need support and an environment they find both nurturing and motivating to help them through the forthcoming period of change. There are number of ways of achieving this, and these are covered in Chapter 8.

B. Efficiency built on repetitive work

Another factor which makes change more difficult to implement at the base of the hierarchic structure is that those jobs rely quite often on the repeated execution of a specific sub-process or procedure; such as order capture, accounts receivable, order picking, merchandising activities etc. Over time, individuals become highly efficient. Their key measurement of performance – and therefore of their self-esteem from a professional point of view – is speed and accuracy. Change the rules of the game, the step sequences of a procedure, or the data that needs to be managed, and these previously high performing individuals will need to suffer the pain of undergoing a new learning curve. This means that for a period of time they will be slower than they were accustomed to be, and will be prone to making mistakes, both of which are a source of de-motivation and frustration for those who prided themselves on being the most efficient in the team.

Clarifying expectations will go a long way towards alleviating these people's frustration and loss of self-esteem: let them know that they need to anticipate a period of re-adjustment, that the Company is aware they will not be able to be as efficient in the early days following the introduction of the new methods, systems or processes. Reiterate why over time these will be more efficient than those currently in use, once everyone has grown accustomed to the new way of doing things. And align expectations regarding the time-span over which these individuals are expected to reach those efficiency levels in the future environment. The Key Performance Indicator during that period of change will not only be speed and accuracy, which will have dipped at first compared to earlier levels, but also the rate of improvement over time until the new systems and procedures are truly embedded in the business.

C.   Reversing learnt behaviours and brand allegiance

Last, but certainly not least, field sales personnel will also experience difficulties in adapting to the rules and ways of working for the future integrated organisation, in spite of being led in most companies by managers who have proven leadership skills and can act as good coaches and motivators. This is because the integration of the two companies' product portfolios may force everyone in the sales team to sing the praise of products or services that they will have compared unfavourably with their own portfolio in previous discussions with their clients. While this is not much of a problem if the two integrating companies' products or services were complimentary to each other, it can become a serious issue if they were previously head-on competitors. When Grand Metropolitan's wine and spirits arm IDV merged with Guinness's United Distillers, I remember a salesman exclaiming in total disbelief: *"I've been selling Johnnie Walker all these years and getting customers to switch from J&B to our brand, you're not now going to ask me to sell J&B to those same people are you?"*. Well yes, this is precisely what was expected of them, but not overnight, and only after a good amount of training and regular coaching from their regional managers.

What this means is that in most cases 'product training' will need to cover more than the mere attributes of the products or services the future company will be selling, to also encompass an understanding of the 'brand values' and the 'essence' of those brands. This will allow the individuals to build the same emotional bond with these new additions to their offering as they have towards their current range. Omitting to convey these would result in people, particularly in the Sales Force, having their 'favourites' within their range and neglecting the others, thereby failing to capture the potential benefits that the merger or acquisition was planning to deliver.

Gathering the detail from those who know

We have just seen that the people who have the most fragmented and yet most detailed knowledge about the two businesses that are about to merge are those team or local managers who are one level above the base of the hierarchical structure. They are the people who are likely to be faced with the highest and most persistent levels of resistance from the individuals in the teams they manage, whose work routines have been turned up-side down, who are having difficulty adapting to the new requirements, and who will be de-motivated by their slower pace of work and reduced accuracy. Unless you show particular consideration for these team leaders and tie them into the integration process from the onset, theirs is the level at which the implementation of your integration programme will derail.

Conversely, there are ways in which you can benefit from the knowledge, influence and large numbers of these team leaders across the business and end up implementing an integration that not only looks good on the drawing board, but will also actually result in an efficient and well thought-through organisation that meets your merger's business case. And you will achieve this by ensuring that once you have pulled together the 'big picture' of your future organisation and started re-designing its processes, you include a panel of team leaders into the relevant work stream of your integration team for a 'walk-through' to test out in detail how these processes will actually work. You will then get a very clear and detailed view of what needs to change, what might be more difficult to change, but also and mainly an inventory of little crass details you might have overlooked and which could jeopardize your plan. At this point, you can still take corrective action and sort out those small but important details that will make a world of difference when the integration takes place. You will have closed that very important gap – sometimes small and yet so crucial – between what looks good on paper and what will work in practice. That gap may be in the design of the process itself, or in the way you propose to implement it.

Beyond using that panel of team leader experts in your integration teams, you also need to ensure that everyone in the organisation is aware that these experts of detail are on board. This is a very powerful way of avoiding the very noxious feeling that can easily spread across organisations in times of profound change that "those guys at the top have no idea of what things are *really* like". Now you have some people who definitely *do* understand how things work (or worked) in real life, and who will have had an opportunity to provide their input into how best to achieve the desired outcome of the integration. What you absolutely want to avoid is the belief that "this will not work, but they didn't bother asking us" or even worse after the event, the ultimate sign of non-involvement: "told you it would never work".

This brings me to another very important aspect about the involvement of the team leader experts in the integration process, not only those who may be included in the work stream teams of your programme, but the entire community of team leaders across the two businesses. Let us remember these are the people who will face daily objections and will have to manage individuals who are struggling to adapt to the new organisation's ways of working. Make sure you have some mechanism to capture their questions and concerns and, very importantly, be certain that they are aware that you have listened to their input and understood it. Their input, ideas and suggestions may not match the vision and aspirations of your business integration, but this is beside the point. What really matters is that they will not feel the frustration that would result from implementing an organisation that disregarded their knowledge and input. For this purpose, you need to capture their input and ideas, make sure they know you have listened to them and understood their point, and that their input was taken into consideration when designing the future organisation and the detail of its processes and systems. There may be very valid reasons for which the chosen organisation design, processes and systems will not be those that the team leader experts had recommended or would have preferred, but the key is to be able to understand where exactly the gaps lie between your solution and theirs, address these gaps, discuss what the alternatives were and be able to explain the pros and cons of the company's decision. And this is possibly the biggest learning I have derived when integrating or transforming organisations and from other examples I have observed around me: most individuals are mature enough to 'agree to disagree', but nobody will find it acceptable to have been overlooked and dismissed.

Capturing the input from team leaders will provide you with invaluable information, a reality check for your plans, but it will also, importantly, involve this essential population of 'doers' into your integration programme and prevent your plans from being perceived as some form of consultant-driven intellectual exercise. It will be your way of proving that you understand that the devil is in the detail and that you value the knowledge of the team leader experts, and this can only be a strong source of reassurance and motivation for those people in your organisation who are 'at the coalface'. Remember that they represent the largest numbers in your overall staff, it is at their level that your organisation mostly interfaces with its environment, and failing to get them on board is likely to cause the failure of the best laid plans.

Lastly, once all has been explained and discussed and there is a feeling of mutual understanding - even if the plan forward does not correspond to some of the stakeholders' personal preference - it will be necessary to obtain an explicit acceptance to follow the plan, rather than just assume that everyone is on board, willingly or reluctantly.

> *Most individuals are mature enough to 'agree to disagree', but nobody will find it acceptable to have been overlooked and dismissed.*

It is quite possible, and even likely, that some individuals will initially declare their intention to follow the plan but will subsequently show resistance. I mentioned above that *most* people can 'agree to disagree', which means also that you are likely to be confronted to a few individuals who simply cannot be converted and will resist your plan no matter how hard you try to demonstrate its logic, advantages and value. Anticipating resistance well in advance will help you decide what stance you will adopt with the various categories of resistors. This will depend very much on the degree of influence a change resistor might have within the company and this is not necessarily linked to hierarchy levels: some long-time employee on the shop-floor might be regarded by his colleagues as a wise man whose opinions are respected. It might be that an in-depth one-to-one conversation with some of those individuals can provide them with additional clarity and alleviate their fears or apprehension. For others, there may be no adequate way of promoting acceptance for the required changes, and it is worth thinking ahead of the time about how these hard-core resistors will be handled, rather than be confronted to an awkward unproductive situation that will require you to improvise at short notice.

In short:

- Listen actively.

- Make sure they know you have listened and understood.

- Explain the background for the decision that was taken and why the alternatives were rejected.

- Acknowledge their input and demonstrate an understanding of the detailed impact the company's decision will have on the transition from today's companies to the desired integrated organisation.

- Obtain explicit acceptance to follow the plan.

- Anticipate resistance and prepare accordingly.

Shaping the top of the pyramid

Having looked at how to ensure the foundation of your organisation is sound and fully on-board with the integration process, let us consider what needs to happen right at the top, within the Executive team. In large companies, it is likely that at least some of the members of the Executive team will already have lived through one or several business integrations, and therefore know to a certain degree what to expect. In medium or small businesses this will probably not be the case, which means that the Executives going through this for the first time will need to cope with their own anxiety and fear of the unknown in addition to driving the integration in their area of the business. In either case, this can be made much easier if the Executive Team can rapidly become just that: a team.

In the same way that the eggs and oil in the kitchen bowl do not spontaneously blend into a smooth mayonnaise, there is no reason to assume that the individuals nominated to become part of the Executive of the new integrated company will automatically 'gel'. Indeed, in large corporations the people who reach the top tend to be very competitive hard-line achievers, keen to project an image of strong leadership – all of these excellent qualities do not, however, predispose these Executives to express candour or openly admit their lack of knowledge or experience in some areas. Quite to the contrary: if these individuals are brought together without some form of skilful facilitation, they will tend to want to 'profile' themselves and 'gain visibility', and this will delay the emergence of natural patterns of behaviour that characterize an efficient team.

One generally successful way of creating a sense of team identity is to run 'away-days' that provide a facilitated informal environment, allowing the members of the future Executive to get to know each other as individuals and gradually gain a good level of mutual comfort and trust. Only at that point can you be assured that the initial competition between the members of the Executive can really turn into mutual support and cohesive teamwork.

I personally feel that this is an area in which one cannot do too much: fostering a strong sense of camaraderie between the members of the Executive team sends a powerful signal across the whole organisation and helps build a sense of trust between the two companies that are about to integrate into one. Therefore, after the Executive's initial away-days, it is worth investing some time in further nurturing their team spirit during the first months of the integration process to prevent a rapid erosion of that initial positive goodwill.

It will be tempting to 'cut corners' here, because away-days could be perceived as a very time consuming activity at a time when the company is being pressured by many other pressing priorities. If the fundamentals of the team are already in place, the further nurturing of team spirit I just mentioned can be achieved by as little as some informal activity at the close of formal meetings. I have witnessed quite a transformation in the rapport between the members of an Executive team after they had spent a couple of hours together on a sailing boat at the close of one of their monthly review meetings. That short interlude gave everyone a chance to relax in an environment devoid of pressure, engage in conversation and share a laugh. This is all about interacting as human beings, rather than corporate super-heroes. And a strong cohesive team at the helm of the organisation is a non-negotiable prerequisite for a successful integration.

> *This is all about interacting as human beings, rather than corporate super-heroes.*

In Essence...

▋ *Articulate the strategic intent to make it palatable and relevant: why are we doing this, benefit to each category of stakeholder, 'what's in it for me'.*

▋ *Check the pulse: seek feedback.*

▋ *Break audiences down into small groups for more open dialogue, feedback and questions; take these small groups into consideration when laying out the communications plan.*

▋ *Saying "I don't know" demonstrates openness and is preferable to giving a wrong or biased response; but follow-up on those questions you could not answer.*

▋ *Use the agenda of regular business meetings to communicate about the integration, placing it in the relevant context of a specific business unit or function.*

▋ *Team leads are an essential population of 'doers' and can be your most powerful change agents; make sure they will be well placed to support the people who report to them during the integration phase: listen to their feedback and suggestions, make sure they know you have understood them, keep them informed and involved, provide a rationale for any decisions that may not please them.*

▋ *Rapidly build a sense of team identity at the top of the organisation.*

Structure and Organisation

Ring fencing the P&L

Defining everyone's area of focus

A few fundamentals need to be clarified from the onset when setting up the structure of the project teams that will be given the task of driving the integration process.

Freeing up people to work on a project is always a challenge. Freeing up *good* people from daily business to join a project team is even more painful. We all know that. The real problem is that the only way to avoid that pain is either to allocate the wrong people to the project, in other words not the *best* people, or to require the best people to work on the project while maintaining their responsibilities in daily work. Experience tells us that either of these easy ways out will lead the integration project to failure or will, at the very least, cause the project's timeline to stretch, resulting in significant costly over-runs and additional strain on the business. So if you do not feel any pain as a result of pulling the team members off their daily duties in the business, assume you are doing something wrong and don't have the best people on the team!

There are two excellent reasons for which, with rare exceptions, the people working on the integration project should be freed from all or at least a large majority of their responsibilities in day-to-day business. The first reason is that the integration work itself is a full-time job, sometimes actually feeling like *more* than a full-time job, and therefore it is unreasonable to assume that the same individual can do both. The second reason, beyond what one might consider to be an acceptable workload, is that when priority conflicts occur or a temporary workload peak hits, invariably it is the integration work that will suffer or be delayed because day-to-day business cannot wait. And so the integration process will begin to drag on, energy levels in the organisation will drop, costs will rise, and the signs of failure will begin to appear…

Conversely, repeatedly distracting those in charge of daily-business with integration-related matters will result in a lack of focus, precisely at a time when it is important for everyone in both companies to keep their eye on the ball and make sure the businesses meet their targets. The very worst thing that can happen during the integration process is for the companies' commercial performance to start slipping, because this can spark off a downward spiral effect as everyone – starting with the shareholders – begins to doubt that the organisation has the ability to come through the integration process unscathed and emerge as a stronger, better consolidated business upon the project's conclusion. It does not take long for a loss in market share, missed big contracts or delays in new product launches to undermine morale in a company and for the blame for all of the company's problems to be laid on the integration process. Any such slippage would call for urgent remedial action, the Executive will need to get 'all hands on deck', and the integration will grind to a temporary halt until the business is back on track. However, as we saw earlier, it takes a lot of energy and skill to build the momentum needed for a major business integration, and it would be hard to imagine that this initial spirit and enthusiasm can be repeated if poor business performance requires the integration to be put on hold, even only once.

A key feature of successful integrations is that they manage to maintain that dual focus: business as usual on the one hand, integration on the other. They prevent the mutual interference between those two areas of focus, and the simplest and most effective means of achieving this clear segregation is to allocate the respective responsibilities to distinct individuals. The challenge is therefore, in parallel to the existing structure of the two organisations in charge of day-to-day business, to set up a structure of high-calibre individuals who can drive the integration while minimizing the interference with those in charge of earning the company's daily bread and butter, and who can at the end of the project be meaningfully redeployed into the integrated organisation. Sourcing that structure is a complex task that is discussed in detail in Chapter 4 'Selecting the Team'.

Achieving that dual focus has a number of implications, which will be addressed in the rest of this chapter.

Starting at the Top

With the exception of the Executive, who have ultimate accountability for business results but also need to make or approve the fundamental decisions and choices underlying the integration process, successfully managing the dual focus of business and integration requires people through the next layers of the companies' hierarchies to be assigned either to 'daily business' or to the integration project, thus avoiding wherever possible having one individual straddling both. And because the members of the Executive cannot be allocated solely to the integration project or to daily business and that the latter will take precedence when the pressure of work builds up, the best practice is to have someone join the Executive in a temporary function of Integration Director, whose sole responsibility is to drive the integration process across the whole business. In this way, the segregation of the two focus areas is assured through the entire organisation.

In most cases, the Integration Director is unlikely to be a pre-existing member of the Executive, because most roles in an Executive team cannot be put on hold for the duration of the integration project. Many companies would be tempted to give this role to their Financial Director, but this is not advisable because the workload of the Finance function becomes huge during the business integration as legal entities are merged or transformed, accounts are merged, financial systems are overhauled, and new management accounts are set up. Usually, this heavy workload requires temporary contractors to be brought into the company to deal with the temporary surge of activity. This is, therefore, clearly not the time to remove the Executive Financial Director from his or her functional role to take on the overall management of the integration project, because this person needs to be fully accountable for the deliverables of the Finance department(s) across the whole business.

The same reasoning would apply to a Human Resources Director, who would naturally be inclined to take on responsibility for driving the integration project, but whose department is one of the most affected by the integration itself and will also in many cases require additional temporary resources during the transition phase.

Consequently, only roles within the Executive team, such as that of a Strategy Director, that do not have a 'hands-on' role in daily business, actually lend themselves to taking on the temporary sole responsibility for the integration project. In the absence of such an individual, a good solution is to provisionally appoint someone one level below the Executive to join the team as Integration Director, or to hire an external interim senior individual to fill this role for the duration of the project. Using an external interim manager presents the important advantage of providing a sense of 'neutrality' in the integration process, and the fact that this temporary role is by definition destined to disappear means that the Integration Director poses no threat to other senior individuals in terms of their own longer-term career aspirations. I like to think of this role as being 'bio-degradable': do a good job and disappear without leaving any ugly traces... In addition, companies that choose to seek an external contractor to join them to lead the integration effort can base their choice of individual on the experience this person has of previous integrations. This is very important given that in many, if not most cases, none of the members of the Executive will have any detailed experience of what a business integration entails. Bringing in expert knowledge for the duration of the project can make the difference between success and failure.

If the Integration Director is selected from within the upper ranks of the organisation, make sure he or she is flanked by an expert who has ample experience of similar integration programmes. Conversely, if the Integration Director role is given to someone who is brought into the organisation as a temporary contractor, it imperative that this contractor be perceived as a person who belongs to the company, and not as a 'consultant', because the impetus to integrate must come from within the organisation and not be perceived as an external imposition. In either case, the absolute pre-requisite is to have someone who already enjoys or can rapidly acquire a high standing in the company, with excellent leadership and communication skills, high levels of emotional resilience, and boundless energy.

Clarifying the boundary between business and integration

Having accepted the idea that accountabilities need to be segregated between business and integration, the necessary step to make this actionable is to ensure that the achievements of both of the focus areas remain measurable and do not mutually impact upon one another.

Business integration is a disruptive and costly exercise: the surge of activity during the transition phase requires a number of contractors to be brought into the company temporarily, in addition to the expensive consultants and advisors that are usually needed to shape the project's blueprint and provide input on specific business or technical aspects of the integration. Significant costs can also be associated with the internal staff allocated to the project team because in many instances travel and hotel accommodation may be needed for a relatively large proportion of them. In spite of the fact that one of the goals of the integration team is to minimize the disruption they cause to daily business while driving their project, occasionally the integration will require staff working on the day-to-day business to perform a number of activities related to the integration programme.

Running the daily business during a period of integration is all but easy, and it will be necessary for the Executive to maintain an appropriate amount of pressure to ensure that business objectives are reached. Therefore everything must be done to avoid the integration from being invoked as an excuse for poor performance. The first step towards this is to require that all integration-related costs be re-charged to the integration budget, to prevent the business results from being unfairly burdened by the integration project. This means that the staff allocated to the project teams should be cross-charged, as well as the travel and accommodation costs they incur. Parallel to that, clear 'Key Performance Indicators' (KPIs) must be in place to measure business performance on the one hand, and the progress of the integration on the other hand. Make sure those KPIs are harmonised from the onset between the two companies to prevent any unwanted trade-offs or window dressing from blurring the performance measurements. More than at any other time in the life of a business, constantly keeping a finger on the pulse of the company is essential in times of integration to keep both the business and the integration project on the rails. Giving those KPIs a high profile throughout the organisation will generate and maintain the appropriate level of focus and determination to succeed.

From the moment a merger or major acquisition is announced till the time when the organisations can be considered as fully integrated, the business undergoes constant scrutiny from its shareholders and possibly the broader financial community. Living up to expectations and fulfilling the promise are both essential. Ring-fencing the P&L and protecting business performance from the adverse impacts of the integration process is an absolute necessity, failing which the pressure for daily business to achieve its targets will cause the integration to abort.

Structure and governance

The general principles

For many people, the very notions of 'programme structure and governance' reflect the typical project manager's obsession with process, order and control: "yet another PowerPoint® chart with boxes and arrows…" some will be thinking! In the case of a venture that includes as many moving parts as is the case of the integration of two companies, you need to believe me when I say that programme structure and governance will have a huge impact not only on the speed with which the integration will take place, but equally on the quality of the final outcome. There are three main reasons behind this:

▪ The integration will call for numerous important decisions to be made, rapidly.

▪ Many decisions require cross-functional input, as a result of which having access to the appropriate levels of authority and knowledge in the relevant functions is of paramount importance.

▪ We have seen that the integration project operates alongside the daily business rather than within it, and therefore clear reporting rules and accountabilities need to be set to ensure that the integration project remains focused on reaching its objectives and delivering the business case that justified the merger or acquisition.

The first step, as in any project of some magnitude, will of course be to appoint the members of the Steering Committee, or Programme Board, who need to have sufficient seniority to be held accountable for the outcome of the integration.

The purpose of this book is not to describe in any detail the roles of governance and structure since these are well documented in a number of methodologies that describe in detail how effective projects and programmes should be run. One of most comprehensive is probably PRINCE-2®, which was developed for the British Department of Trade and Industry and is now applied as the standard for large programmes in a number of countries across the world. The level of rigour that needs to be applied to the integration programme will, of course, depend on the anticipated complexity of the programme: integrating a few operating units spread across two or three countries will not require the same level of procedural thoroughness than the merger of two multinational corporations.

The specialised Project Management literature concentrates on roles, responsibilities, procedures and reporting lines, all of which apply when running an integration. However, what also matters crucially in the specific case of a company integration is to understand the impact the structure of the project teams will have.

Organising the teams by outcomes, not by function

To ensure that all the functions impacted by the business integration are represented on the project, many companies do what appears to be the most obvious and natural thing i.e. set up a project team that is divided into work streams each representing one of the company's functions: Sales, Marketing, Finance, H.R., Manufacturing and so on. The alternative way of organising the work streams would be to group people into task-forces each responsible for a specific set of *outcomes*, such as 'Product Range', 'Office Locations', 'Organisation Design' etc.

Having led integration projects using both of these two project team structures, my preference very clearly goes to having the teams clustered by *Outcome* rather than by *Function*. The reason for this is that the very *raison d'être* of the integration project team is to plan, design and implement everything that would not otherwise occur automatically within the organisation's various functions.

Remember my analogy with the eggs sitting in a bowl, which do not spontaneously blend with the oil and turn into mayonnaise! Most of the big decisions that are required to blend two organisations into a single effective seamless company call upon the input of several functions. The Human Resources function cannot decide single-handedly on the design of the new organisation. Combining the portfolio of products or services of the two companies into a future integrated offering requires the input from Sales, Marketing, Strategy, Manufacturing, Finance and Information Systems. The purpose of the integration project team is precisely to bring representation of these functions around a table to analyse, understand, decide, plan and execute the changes that are required to make the two companies evolve into one.

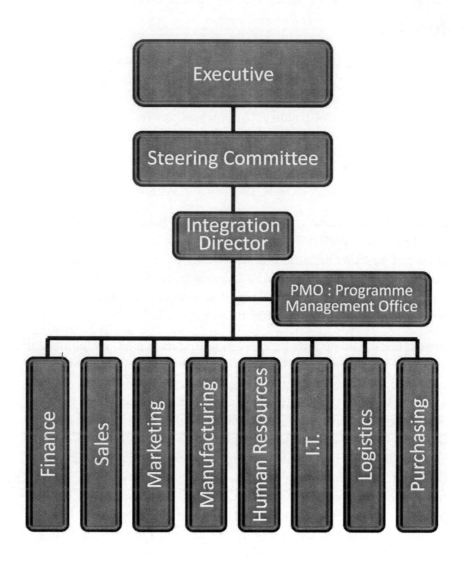

Functional project team structure

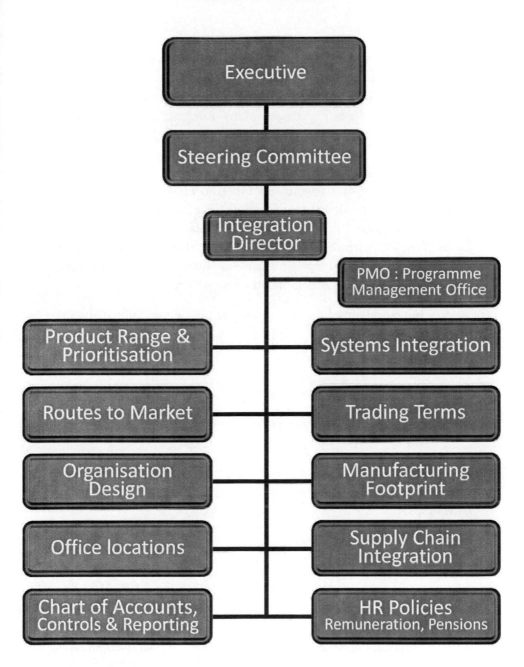

Outcomes based project team structure

One could of course argue that the same can be achieved by structuring the project team around functional work streams, and indeed this is true, as the collective knowledge of the project team and its access to information depends on the selection of team members rather than the structure of the work groups. Many integrations are run using function-based project teams, some of them with the support of some of the world's leading auditing and consultancy firms, and therefore it would not be honest of me to state that a function-based project team cannot succeed. I recently had to lead an integration that was precisely structured along these function-based principles, and we did succeed. But things could have been easier. Having worked with both forms of project team structures, I believe that the 'Outcomes' oriented structure presents four very significant advantages when compared to the more conventional 'Functional' team structure:

- Improved opportunity for lateral thinking and radical change.

- Better detection and management of functional interdependencies.

- Single point of ownership for key deliverables and decisions.

- Reduced complexity in organising and managing the project work.

Let me share with you what I have been able to observe in terms of the impact the project team structure can have in relation to the points listed above:

Lateral thinking and radical change

Functional teams merely mirror what already exists in the organisation: their thinking and perception of the business will be a subset of their respective department's knowledge and experience. In the absence of the constant input from other functions around them, they will tend to think in silos, and are likely to strive for an optimisation of their function rather than optimize the way the company's core processes flow across the organisation's functional barriers. Working in a functional team also gives the team members less exposure and fewer learning opportunities.

By contrast, unlike functional teams, outcome-based teams are a microcosm of the business that gives the team members an end-to-end view and understanding of how the company operates today and how differently it could operate in the future. That structure allows them to envisage bold change without a fear of unsuspected impacts elsewhere in the business, as all the interested parties are represented in the team.

Detection and management of functional interdependencies

Functional project teams developing their plans must constantly reach out to the other teams to identify interdependencies and review their progress to ensure they remain synchronised during the implementation of the integration. This is much easier to manage if each stream already comprises representation from all the functions required to produce a given set of deliverables: all the people and knowledge required can then be sat at the same table.

Ownership for key deliverables and decisions

Companies that opt for a function-based team structure will designate 'owners' for each core process and then allocate the responsibility for integrating that process to the relevant function. They might, for example, ask the Marketing work stream to define the consolidated portfolio of goods or services that the future integrated company will sell. Or should that responsibility be given to the Sales work stream? The reality is that a number of functions need to be involved to make such a complex decision, and this places the burden on one function to coordinate its work with all of the others. Furthermore, the impartiality of the recommendations made by a function-based team may be questionable. For example, a team of Sales people will not be inclined to streamline the portfolio because this requires culling some products that sell quite successfully but which may cause other issues in the organisation in terms of manufacturing processes or supply chain complexity.

Outcomes-based project team structures overcome this problem as each work stream includes representation of all the functions whose input is required to formulate balanced recommendations and oversee their implementation. There is no risk of one particular function subsequently saying: "this is not what we wanted".

Complexity in organising and managing the project work

Outcomes-based project teams do not need to repeatedly run cross-functional workshops to coordinate their work while analysing, re-designing or rolling-out processes across the integrated organisation. This greatly simplifies the work of the Integration Director's project management team. The only coordination that is required with outcomes-based team structures is the identification at the onset of the project and inclusion in the initial project plan of interdependencies between key milestones or deliverables. For example, the portfolio of products or services needs to be defined before deciding how best to sell them and finalising the design of the sales organisation. In large integration projects, a few 'check-points' will be needed to determine whether any new interdependencies have arisen as a result of the evolution of the integration work.

By opposition, in function-based project teams, information needs to iterate between the work streams, approvals take more time and often require the sequential circulation of documents between the various functional groups involved, cross-functional coordination becomes a continuous task and a source of many arbitration issues, which often need to be escalated to the project's steering committee, causing further delays. Whereas a single cross-functional outcome-oriented workgroup could manage these steps single-handedly.

Small organisations setting up outcome-based work streams will find that a number of individuals will belong to more than one work stream. This will reduce the work streams' flexibility in scheduling workshops and other such meetings to avoid diary clashes, but I still believe the benefits of the outcome-driven structure are worth the effort, because the work streams remain more focused, progress faster and remain fully accountable for their deliverables.

The advantage of an outcome-based project team structure over a functional structure is particularly clear in large organisations that span many locations or several countries because the key issue is one of communication, which is exacerbated by size and geographical distance.

In the case of small companies, it may be that all of the individuals involved in the integration project have frequent opportunities of being together and discussing ongoing issues relating to the integration project, in which case the risk of working in parallel functional silos is not as great as it would be in a large complex organisation. But let us not be fooled into thinking that cross-functional work is complex only in large multi-nationals. I have seen a medium size company whose entire project team only comprised some thirty individuals organised in functional teams seriously struggle to integrate and rationalise its product range or formulate a clear recommendation on office locations. The examples below illustrate why the complexity of the decision-making process is not necessarily linked to the size of the organisation.

Outcome-based teams in practice: a few examples

Integrating the product range

Let us start with the integration of the product range or portfolio of services that I mentioned earlier. A quick look at the key steps that are required to integrate two product portfolios easily highlights the extent to which not only the input from other functions than Sales is required, but also some form of ground rules to allow a coherent resolution of priority conflicts, in the absence of which the project team will end up 'negotiating' the maintenance or culling of each product in the portfolio, one by one.

The actual steps of the integration process will vary depending on the business sector, and the functions involved will depend on the actual remit of each of these functions, which can differ from one company to another. The example below is shown here for illustrative purposes only.

PRODUCT PORTFOLIO INTEGRATION		
Step	**Description**	**Functions involved**
Agreeing common definitions	Definition of common criteria: • Performance measurement • Product classification definitions • Market segmentation definitions	Sales Marketing Strategy Finance Manufacturing Supply Chain
Analysis of historical performance	Performance and SWOT analysis (by product or product category)	Sales Marketing Finance
Building a model of the market	Definition of market target and competitive set Product / category life-cycle model	Strategy Marketing
Define a model of user behaviour	User clustering according to affinity for product categories and brands, Characteristics of non-users, light users, average users, heavy users New user recruitment model	Strategy Marketing
Target definition	Definition of success criteria (what it takes to beat the competition)	Sales, Marketing, Strategy, Finance, Manufacturing

Step	Description	Functions involved
Establishing strategic priorities and focus	Prioritisation of products within the integrated company's strategy	Sales, Marketing, Strategy, Finance
Portfolio integration Product prioritisation	Establish common product hierarchies, product and parts numbering, naming conventions, impacts on tooling and production equipment, product costing, pricing, product knowledge training manuals, training schemes for sales and marketing	Sales Marketing Manufacturing Supply Chain Information Systems Finance
Reducing complexity	Portfolio rationalisation: identify products that will be discontinued i.e product duplication or substitutions; insufficient direct and indirect profit contribution	Sales Marketing Manufacturing Supply Chain Finance
Adapting the manufacturing footprint	As a consequence of the newly-defined streamlined portfolio, what do we manufacture where? What impact does this have on the location and relative size of our production plants? This may need to loop back to the work developed by the 'Portfolio integration / product prioritisation' work stream.	Manufacturing Finance Human Resources Supply Chain IT (Data)

The table above clearly shows that representation from several functions is repeatedly required throughout the product portfolio integration process. Devolving this responsibility to a single function, in this case most probably Marketing, would create the risk that some aspects that are relevant to other functions will be overlooked or misunderstood. This can lead to a multiplication of bilateral discussions between functions, whereas an outcome-based work stream would always have all the information required at hand to make decisions and progress the work.

In a company that structured its integration team in functional streams, I have seen the Marketing work stream agonise over the difficulty of establishing a common product hierarchy, which required their work to be synchronised with inputs from Information Systems, Sales, Finance (because of the implications on management accounting) and Manufacturing. In this particular case, it took them almost eight months to integrate the portfolio and be ready to start the rationalisation, whereas this should have been possible in anything between three and five months if a cross-functional outcome-oriented work stream had been given this task.

Selecting the future office locations

Some other cross-functional interdependencies are less obvious than in the above example. Think of the connection between human resources and information systems. Imagine a team responsible for deciding on the location of offices. In a project structured around functional teams, it is likely the responsibility for deciding the criteria for site selection and implementing the office moves would be given to the Human Resources department. If the two companies that are about to merge are located in different cities, the choice between moving to location A or location B will be influenced by a number of factors, some of which are within the remit of the Human Resources function, such as the ability to recruit and retain talent, the number of people who are likely to be made redundant as a result of the move to one location, etc.

But in practice, when choosing between the office locations of two merging companies, the decision may also be influenced by the computer platform that has been selected for the future business. This is because vacating the premises of the company that is using that system today would cause the loss of all staff in key functions, such as customer service, order management, finance or purchasing, and switching the staff of the business's core functions to a new software platform may be deemed to be too risky amidst all the other changes that occur during the merger.

Selecting sales tools

A business integration project provides a good trigger to enhance systems with the aim of improving the company's ability to manage information for better decision making. The systems and tools used by the Sales function are no exception to this, because they are an important component of the business's future growth.

What planning tools should the sales people use? How do we want to monitor their activity? What data should they be able to access? What numeracy and technical skills do we believe they should have? What type of hardware will they need to manage their work? Choosing the optimal system and set of tools is a decision process that requires inputs from a number of functions in the organisation: senior Sales management of course, but also IT, which will need to consider the technical aspects of interfaces, compatibility and maintenance; Finance, which will have a keen interest in the cost and reporting capability of the tools; Marketing, which may want to ensure that the data structures supported by the system can reflect the company's segmentation of the market; and Human Resources, which may be involved in setting up training sessions and will also, in some countries, be involved in a consultation process if changes to technology and support tools are subject to approval by employee representatives. None of the functions listed above has the authority to decide alone what this set of tools and systems should be. In a project structure segmented by Function, it is likely that the ultimate responsibility for this decision will rest with the Sales function, but just as in the previous examples, a cross-functional outcome-based team will provide and implement a recommendation much faster, with a far greater degree of overall commitment and ownership.

In Essence...

▮ *Segregate two areas of focus: daily business versus integration.*

▮ *Clarify the boundaries to safeguard accountability: ensure the integration work does not distort the KPIs of the ongoing business.*

▮ *Business performance must remain under close scrutiny during the integration: keep a finger on the pulse. Any significant downturn in business performance will derail the integration process.*

▮ *Establish clear governance of the integration programme: Steering Committee, Programme Director, team structure, definition of roles and responsibilities, issues resolution process, project management methodology.*

▮ *Organise the project teams by outcomes rather than by function.*

Selecting the Team

A few basic rules

A tough challenge indeed – but not an insurmountable one. Let us consider the criteria that need to be satisfied to enable an orderly integration. I have ranked these in what I perceive to be the decreasing level of priority:

- The daily business must have the resources required to remain on track.

- The integration team must collectively possess detailed knowledge of the entire existing business (or have access to that knowledge) and the capability to envision a different future.

- Members of the integration team that were selected from among existing staff and management must have a medium or long-term future in the integrated company.

- Members of the integration team must be flexible regarding location and working hours for the duration of the integration process; this requires specific attributes in terms of attitude, style, personality, openness to change and emotional intelligence.

- The composition of the integration team should, if at all possible, reflect a balance between the two companies that are integrating, as well as fair representation of those companies' business and geographical cultures.

■ Members of the integration team should be well connected within the organisation.

What the rules mean in practice

Let us take a closer look at the implication of the above criteria.

The daily business must have the resources required to keep on track.

> Safeguarding on-going business performance is an absolute must, and this can best be achieved by a combination of having sufficient resources in place, and of prioritising ruthlessly the activities that are scheduled to take place during the integration period. Most companies have, at any one time, a number of projects that explore various opportunities, but do not contribute to the bottom line in the current financial year. All of these should be subjected to serious review, with the aim of putting as many projects as possible on hold. Doing so will ensure that the organisation remains within the limits of what it can manage and does not deliberately try to exceed its bandwidth, and will also prevent a feeling of 'project mania' from developing. Furthermore, the projects that are temporarily put on ice will free some resources that, hopefully, can then contribute towards the integration effort.

> But the key aim of halting non-essential projects is to maintain focus, to ascertain that meeting the company's commercial objectives never becomes a secondary imperative in the business.

> The kind of individual needed to run the business 'as is' is not the same as the people you need to shape a different future. The resources pulled out of the business to join the integration team will leave gaps in the organisation's structure. In many instances this can be an excellent opportunity to 'stretch' a number of individuals beyond the remits of their current job,

which is both an excellent learning opportunity as well as a chance to assess the individual's development potential *in situ*.

Before pulling resources out of the business, it is essential to consider which individuals must imperatively remain in their roles to ensure the good daily functioning of the company. In practice, most businesses will find it extremely difficult to completely dispense with the input and knowledge of the individuals who are needed for the integration project. Unless several other important projects can be put on hold during the integration, it is unlikely that sufficient internal resources will be available without causing some pain in the organisation. Backfilling the positions made vacant by the integration project's resource drain is quite an art, because these may be fairly senior positions and hiring external contractors to temporarily fill these gaps might not always be the smart answer, particularly when company-specific knowledge is needed to perform the job adequately. But conversely, one needs to very seriously challenge, case by case, the extent to which any individual is truly irreplaceable; too many companies fail to consider all the alternatives, as a result of which the integration project is starved of resources and has no hope of being successful.

As I mentioned earlier, the best practice is very clearly to ensure a split of responsibilities between people working on day-to-day business and those seconded to the integration project. One way of preventing the paralysis of the business when key individuals are temporarily removed from the structure for the duration of the integration is to adopt an 80/20 principle: if a particular individual if required for the integration task force, ask yourself whether someone in his or her team can step into his/her role and at least manage 80% of that person's activity, only requiring some guidance or authorisations for the remaining 20%. This is achievable in the great majority of cases, and it is a good way of facilitating and accelerating the release of excellent resources for the project while minimising the pain to the business, which is important because the integration project needs to kick off with its team fully staffed to maintain momentum and avoid delays.

By adopting this 80/20 principle, the integration project can be articulated around a four-day week, with the fifth day set aside for the members of the integration team to touch base with their backfills in the business, provide guidance and coaching, share knowledge and assist with the resolution of current business issues. This does not contradict the principle of segregation of responsibilities, because the backfill person is accountable for the execution of the work while the members of the integration team concentrate of their project's deliverables, so there is little risk of conflicting priorities having an adverse impact on the business or the project. Another positive aspect of this 80/20 schedule is that the members of the integration team will not feel alienated from the business. Scheduling the debrief/coaching day on Fridays presents the advantage of ending the week with 'a clean slate' – and therefore peace of mind, so that everyone can regenerate during the weekend and be fresh for the start of the next challenging week.

Freeing up the right resources, and freeing them rapidly, is the most important thing the business can do to support the success of the integration project. Companies that have a structured succession planning process in place will know instantly who should backfill for whom. For the other companies – the majority I suspect! – which aspire to having succession plans in place, but unfortunately are not there yet, releasing key talent and organising the backfill is an excellent opportunity to give serious consideration to the development of latent talent. When no suitable backfill can be identified among the people reporting to someone needed on the integration team, consider a 'lateral' backfill from another similar function, or possibly an international temporary secondment if the company can identify suitable candidates in other markets. From the employees' perspective, regardless of whether the secondment is sourced vertically, laterally or internationally, this challenging learning opportunity gives real meaning to the concept of *people development* and can be a strong motivator as it is a tangible sign of the company's trust in an individual's capabilities and potential.

The integration team must collectively possess detailed knowledge of the entire existing business (or have access to that knowledge) and the capability to envision a different future.

Having laid down the principles that will allow the business to survive the strain of the integration transition period, let us turn our attention to the integration project team itself.

Getting the right individuals onto the team is crucial. The definition of the 'right' individuals is dependent on their skill set, knowledge, experience, but is also a function of their personalities. Good preparation and planning (see next Chapter) will identify for each function what skill set or knowledge and experience is required, as well as the likely timing and duration of the need for that resource. In terms of the personalities that best fit this role, a number of attributes come into play. Extrovert individuals who are good team players will tend to be the best contributors; they will need a high level of resilience to stress, flexibility in terms of working hours and travel, and a good knowledge of the organisation to allow them to rapidly know where to find the information they will require along the integration journey.

If you cannot find enough individuals who fulfil the criteria of knowledge and experience and also present the personality traits that would make them ideal candidates for the integration team, do not despair: the vast majority of companies face the same problem. You can circumvent this problem by organising several or all of your work streams in a two-tier structure: a core team of permanent members who possess the personality traits that will make them valuable contributors and problem solvers, and a set of 'subject matter experts' who have in-depth knowledge of the way the company operates today. These subject matter experts will be called upon by the permanent core team members to feed into the integration work as and when needed, and to sense-check and validate some of the integration team's output before implementation.

At this point, you have a list of candidates who fit the profiles of your integration project team. Now begins the delicate process of matching the project roles to specific individuals in the two companies and negotiating their release from day-to-day business. Beware of individuals that the business volunteers to release too easily! Unless those individuals were recently released by another project, or indeed by one of the projects that the integration will have caused to be suspended, there is a risk of staffing the integration team with 'wandering souls' (almost every company has a few of those, even if nobody likes to admit it), and while these people might be very reliable and diligent, they are unlikely to be the dynamic proactive and hard working people who are needed to drive a successful integration. Having said this, these wandering souls could provide a very worthwhile contribution to the business by acting as backfills for other individuals seconded to the integration project.

The people who get seconded to the integration project will be exposed to a very unique experience, because the analysis and re-design of the organisation and its underlying processes will give them a helicopter view across the company that they were unlikely to have in their daily jobs. This gives them a broader understanding of the business and a strong sense of belonging as they will have contributed towards shaping the future integrated company. It is therefore imperative that the largest possible number of people on the integration team have the potential to be meaningfully redeployed into the business upon the completion of the integration project, to fully benefit from this very valuable pool of knowledge.

There is an important distinction between having extensive knowledge and thinking one knows everything... Having very knowledgeable individuals on the integration team can shorten the time required for fact finding and thus allows work to progress fast, but one needs to remind such individuals that even if they feel they know everything about their current role, function and company, the aim of the project is to create a *different* company, which may include a mix of elements from two companies that are about to integrate, or indeed to include some best practice that is currently present in neither company. The ability to keep an open mind and challenge the status quo is therefore an absolute must. This is worth emphasizing, because people can often become quite passionate during discussions in the integration teams and tend to defend their way of working as the only conceivable way.

Individuals who have a wealth of business knowledge but a limited ability for lateral thinking can make excellent subject matter experts to *support* the integration team, rather than permanent members of the integration project who are responsible for *driving* the integration. This presents the advantage of associating them to the integration effort rather than taking the risk of alienating them as a result of disregarding their views and not listening to their comments and recommendations. As mentioned earlier in Chapter 2 ("Gathering the detail from those who know"), most people can accept disagreeing with a decision, but will be very resentful if their input was not sought *prior* to making that decision. Likewise with members of staff you might regard as knowledgeable but stubborn individuals. Appointing them as subject matter experts is a source of motivation and acknowledges their value without restricting the latitude for radical change in the business during the integration process.

Members of the integration team must have a medium or long-term future in the integrated company.

Any company that has gone through the pain and trouble of selecting the best candidates for its integration team and releasing them from the daily business to implement the project will be keen to retain the knowledge and experience they will have gathered during the course of the integration. Retaining company knowledge beyond the integration is crucial. This applies less to positions on the integration team that require specific technical or functional expertise (as opposed to market, business sector or company knowledge), which can be sourced externally with interim contractors or consultants if suitable internal resources cannot be seconded to the project team.

Making it clear from the onset when the integration team is about to be formed that its members are people the company values highly and is keen to retain will inevitably make it easier to attract the right individuals for the task. In the absence of this clear statement of intent, there is always a fair degree of reluctance to join a 'project' that is feared to potentially be a dead-end track of one's career. This is all the truer given that in the rest of the company everyone is jockeying for their position to be retained in the future organisation. Therefore it is essential that the team member candidates do not get the feeling they are being asked to shape a company in which they have no future – quite to the contrary.

Turning the company's good intentions into action is another matter. In the same way it will have been difficult to pull the integration team members away from the daily business, when the new integrated organisation is set up there will inevitably be a strong desire to fill every position as soon as possible. In the case of the integration team members, this will not be possible because their remit in that project team will extend beyond the early days of the new organisation. We shall look at this issue in chapter 11 ("Redeployment"), but for the moment just bear in mind that the guide-lines that will be used to select candidates for the integration team as well as the rules governing their redeployment in the organisation upon completion of the project must be very clear and 'transparent', so that there are no feeling in the company of favouritism or unfair pressures exerted on individuals. Making sure these fair and open rules are known across the organisation will also contribute towards creating the same expectation of fairness and rigour when the integration project reaches the important milestones of organisation design and appointments: this is essential if one wants to maintain a degree of serenity in the business during the project's implementation, in the absence of which the staff dedicated to running the daily business will spend their mental energy worrying about their future rather than being focused on keeping the company's results on track.

Members of the integration team must be flexible regarding location and working hours for the duration of the integration process; this requires specific attributes in terms of attitude, style, personality, openness to change and emotional intelligence.

Because mergers and acquisitions only seldom occur between two companies located in one same town, getting the members of the project team to really work as a team will inevitably require them to travel and spend part of their time in hotel accommodations or some other form of 'campus'. Travel and life in hotel rooms is part of the daily routine of most senior executives, such as those who will have decided to proceed with the acquisition or merger they are about to implement. However, while a salesman expects his job to require a fair degree of travel, most other people in organisations are accustomed to a much more sedentary lifestyle; in many cases the closeness between their home and their workplace may have been one of the reasons for which they had chosen their present role. Do not underestimate the burden this may represent for some individuals and by the same token do not paint a rosy picture to project team candidates. For most of the team members, joining the integration team is at least a one year commitment, if they need to get involved in process design, documentation and training; longer than one year in most large integration programmes if they need to accompany the implementation of the integration in several markets.

The only honest way to present the situation is to admit that this may be a challenge but that the learning and experience they will derive from the project will make the effort worthwhile. If project team candidates are not given the opportunity to think this through, there is a high risk that some of them may ask to be discharged from the project after the first few months. This will send a bad signal through the company, giving the dropout candidates a feeling of failure and deep demotivation. And you will be left with the unforeseen problem of urgently having to find a replacement who will not benefit from the same induction as the original members of the team and will therefore most likely be less efficient on the project.

This is another reason for favouring the 80/20 project team organisation I mentioned earlier, where project work is concentrated on four days per week, as a consequence of which those team members that need to travel to work on the project can expect to spend only three nights away from home on average… and four at home. Psychologically, this can make the burden of travel and hotel nights seem much lighter.

Some personalities are better suited to project life than others. Among the potential candidates, if possible it is preferable to select those individuals who are good team players and have an ability to rapidly build a rapport with the other new members of the team, who thrive on change and accept unpredictability, are resilient to stress and therefore have a good level of emotional intelligence[3].

---

[3] The definition of 'Emotional intelligence' used here is that of the Goleman model (Daniel Goleman, 1998), which includes:

Self-awareness — the ability to read one's emotions and recognize their impact while using gut feelings to guide decisions.

Self-management — involves controlling one's emotions and impulses and adapting to changing circumstances.

Social awareness — the ability to sense, understand, and react to others' emotions while comprehending social networks.

Relationship management — the ability to inspire, influence, and develop others while managing conflict.

The composition of the integration team should if at all possible reflect a balance between the two companies which are integrating, as well as fair representation of those companies' business and geographical cultures.

There are two excellent reasons for seeking to establish a balanced representation that reflects the plurality and diversity of views of the business: the first one has to do with 'perceptions', the second is related to knowledge and ideas.

Unless there is a deliberate desire for one of the companies' culture to be taken-over or overwhelmed by the other's, most mergers like to position themselves as a 'marriage of equals', or at least aspire for the resulting combined integrated business to be the alliance of the best of both constituent companies. This would also apply to most significant acquisitions. But in spite of this, just in the same way as the parents of newly-weds are too often convinced, for no justifiable reason, that their offspring is being led harshly by the other member of the new couple, people in organisations that are about to merge cannot help thinking that their company is about to be conquered and muzzled by the other party to the merger. And far from softening over time, this perception of being the 'victim', the side that is being asked to make all the efforts, tends to increase as the first effects of change become perceptible during the integration process. The comparison with new couples learning to live together is not fortuitous: converging towards a common way of doing things requires efforts, and human nature is such that the efforts we need to make personally occupy a far greater share of mind than those we require from others.

In terms of perceptions, striving to achieve a good balance of representation of the two companies in the composition of the project team therefore makes eminent sense. All the more so that when the team is formed, organisation announcements will be circulating explaining who is on the team and in what capacity, and at that point, in the same way as they will have done it when the composition of the future integrated Board was announced, you can bet that the first reaction of almost everyone reading the announcement will be to identify who is from which company, what 'ratio of power' this represents between the two entities, and begin to hypothesize on what this may mean for the future in the belief that the die is already cast ...

Clearly, with the number of criteria and constraints that need to be considered when selecting candidates for the integration team, one would be very lucky to end up with a ratio close to the ideal 50/50, but bear in mind that if the bias gets close to 1/3 – 2/3 or worse, a very skilful communication exercise will need to take place when the team composition is announced to prevent everyone in the organisation from thinking that there are a 'winner' and a 'loser' in this game. There may be excellent rational reasons for ending up with a team that has one third fewer members from one of the merging organisations, particularly if the companies differ very much in size or if a particular range of skill sets was required. The key is that the majority of the staff in the two organisations must understand why this unbalanced representation is nonetheless fair and justified. Failure to achieve this will mean that acceptance of any changes resulting from the business integration will at best be reluctant.

In large international organisations, including team members from countries other than the one in which the headquarters are located will be helpful in terms of perception. The key aim is to avoid ending up in a situation where staff in other markets feel the integrated solution has been masterminded by headquarters with little understanding or regard for the companies located in other countries. Sadly, this is sometimes the case in international Anglo-Saxon or American companies, because until there is proof to the contrary, staff located in continental Europe, Asia or Latin America will believe that their Anglo-Saxon bosses have very limited knowledge and understanding of their markets' specific needs and circumstances. Having a few team members from markets other than 'Centre' can suffice to give the sense that the voice of those other markets is being heard.

So much for *perceptions*. Let us turn to *knowledge and ideas*, which is the other consideration that justifies the time and difficulty of setting up a balanced project team. The aspiration to build the future business based on the 'best of both' can only materialise if the project team has enough access to the detailed knowledge and ideas emanating from the two organisations, either directly or because someone on the team is keen for these to be put on the table for consideration by the team. And beyond aiming for that 'best of both', the in-depth change and transformation required to integrate two companies is the best possibility to also introduce new ideas that go well beyond the 'best of both' and draw upon best practice observed in other companies. An integration team that comprises too large a proportion of participants from one of the parties to the merger will inevitably tend to strive to create a company that is 'more of the same but bigger'. This fails to capture the benefits that this unique opportunity offers in terms of step-change improvements in the efficiency and agility of the resulting business.

If the availability of suitable candidates for the core-team of the integration project is such that the ratio of representation from the two companies is significantly imbalanced, there is an opportunity to improve the picture, particularly in terms of knowledge and ideas, by drawing on a number of subject matter experts from the 'under-represented' company, who will be able to fill the gap during brain-storming sessions and workshops run within the integration project.

Members of the integration team should be well connected within the organisation.

Compared to individuals who are relatively unknown in an organisation, team members who have a good network of contacts in the organisation can gather information faster because they know who can supply them with what they need and will generally obtain quicker responses from the people to whom they send information requests. But the other reason for trying to include a few influencers in the various work groups of the integration team is that these people will become invaluable when change begins to be implemented throughout the organisation. The more influential and well networked members of the integration team will become key levers of the stakeholder management effort throughout the implementation phase, because their deep involvement in the preparation and realisation of the integration gives them the right level of credibility in the eyes of the rest of the company's employees.

In Essence...

▋ *Appoint existing internal staff to the integration teams whenever possible when company or sector knowledge is needed: these people will retain the knowledge in the company when the integration is over.*

▋ *Select the brightest people for the integration teams: these are the people who not only have a good knowledge of the business as it currently stands, but also have the capability of envisaging a different feature, other ways of working, other paths that can lead to the realisation of the Company's strategic objectives.*

▋ *Be aware of the personality traits that are required for project team members to successfully endure the prolonged strain of the integration: people who lack these are likely to drop out of the project or leave the company, hindering the progress of the integration process.*

▌ *Freeing up the right resources rapidly is the most important thing the business can do to support the integration project.*

▌ *Do not starve the organisation of the resources it needs to conduct day-to-day business. Backfill the vacant positions, either by broadening the remit of existing staff and providing them with a valuable learning opportunity, or by hiring interim staff and contractors.*

▌ *Set up a two-tier project team structure: permanent members dedicated to the project, and subject matter experts who may be called upon on occasions to provide input or run a detailed reality check where in-depth specific business knowledge is required.*

▌ *Give serious consideration from the onset of the integration as to how the team members will be redeployed into the business at the end of the programme: this is crucial to avoid a loss of business knowledge.*

Preparation and Planning

Starting early

Now that we have a clearer idea of what type of individual would make a good candidate for the project team and how the integration team can be structured, we need to consider how soon the project team can and should be defined and set-up. The sooner the better is the obvious answer to that question. What people tend to overlook, however, is the fact that a lot of preparation can take place even *before* the acquisition transaction has taken place or approval for the merger has been received from the relevant trade commission authorities. There are of course very stringent legal rules that govern what information two companies can or cannot discuss and exchange, and these need to be adhered to scrupulously.

On the other hand, let us remember that 'speed matters'. As soon as the Regulators have given their approval to a major acquisition or merger, the shareholders and the market at large will expect things to get moving pretty soon. Nominating a project team and freeing its members from the daily business can be a lengthy process. Gathering all the information that will be required to ensure the project kicks off at a fast pace as soon as the Regulators have given their green light can be a very long process too. Consequently, the more you can prepare ahead of Day One, the better.

I would actually go one step further and contend that this early preparation is essential to ensure that the integration project team is correctly resourced, because unless you know well in advance which areas of the business will be easy to integrate and which others will present a serious challenge, it is most unlikely the project team will comprise individuals with the appropriate skill-set and experience or that it will be sufficiently resourced to tackle some very specific areas of great complexity or difficulty. Unexpected needs for specialised resources once the project has already gathered momentum are likely to delay the implementation, as such resources are very seldom available at short notice, and assigning them to the project without any transition time will cause disruption elsewhere in the business.

Starting what?

How much preparation can take place in advance of Day One depends on a number of factors, one of them being the likelihood that the merger or acquisition transaction will actually take place. If there is a high risk that the Regulators will oppose the transaction, there may be some reluctance to invest time, effort and money in working on a project that will never materialize. And yet, most companies do not think twice about investing important sums of money and resources in new product development, when we all know that only a minority of new products turn out to be real successes. A merger or major acquisition should be viewed in the same way: a possible opportunity for the company to leap forward, in the same way it would if it were to launch a product that turns out to be a real market hit.

The more risk-averse reader may prefer to consider the preparation work ahead of Day One as a means of defining more accurate budgets and securing an orderly execution of the integration. Carrying out some in-depth advance preparation work ahead of Day One is like knowing what topics will be included in an exam ahead of sitting the test. Who in their right mind would renounce such an opportunity of scoring good marks?

But how do you get to know what questions will be asked in an exam? Cheating is not acceptable, and is indeed harshly punished when it comes to companies that are about to merge or buy each other out. There is very specific legislation in most countries that emphasizes the need for the candidates to a merger to continue operating as competitors until the day they have a common owner, the famous Day One. Without going into the intricacies of the various legislations, let us consider the spirit of these laws. The basic idea underlying all of them is that two companies that are about to merge or otherwise have a common owner are not allowed to discuss topics or disclose information that they would not feel comfortable sharing with their other competitors. In this information age, a lot of facts and figures are freely available to the public, particularly when it comes to publicly quoted companies. But even if we consider private companies, the location of their offices, approximate number of staff per location, and other such factors are not trade secrets. Likewise, other elements of information that are probably not published do not represent commercially sensitive data and it would not really matter if other competitors knew about them; for example what software platform a company uses to run its business.

Taking a serious look at all openly available information and data can already provide an outline of the integration work that will be required. A clearer picture will emerge from the data collected during the due diligence process that will have preceded the decision to apply for an authorisation to merge or proceed with a major acquisition. Most companies do not even make full use of that information prior to the kick-off of their integration project, and this is a very unfortunate missed opportunity.

But unlike school exams, there is a way of finding out much more about the forthcoming challenges when dealing with a company merger or acquisition, and the reason for this is that whereas students cannot send someone else to sit their exam, in mergers and acquisitions part of the preparation work can be delegated to a third party. That third party needs to guarantee a high degree of neutrality and maintain a 'firewall' between the two companies that are about to merge. This is where large auditing companies or serious consultancy practices come into play. We all know their services don't come cheap, but using their resources for some in-depth pre-merger data analysis can be enormously valuable. The results of that preparation work will give the integration project a head start, allowing it to rapidly gain momentum, which will be very motivating and will strongly energize the members of the integration project team.

> *Carrying out some in-depth advance preparation work ahead of Day One is like knowing what topics will be included in an exam ahead of sitting the test*

When Guinness and Grand Metropolitan merged in 1997 to form what is today Diageo, inordinate precautions were taken to ensure that no commercially sensitive information would be discussed, even inadvertently, whenever meetings involving participants from both companies prior to the day the merger transaction actually took place. Representatives from the legal advisors attended the meetings to certify that these had been conducted in accordance with the requirements of the legislation, and also to blow a whistle if conversations got anywhere close to even alluding to information that might be considered as commercially sensitive. However, during that same time, considerable amounts of information were being gathered by the companies' advisors, primarily by McKinsey, which gave very clear clues as to how the integration would need to be designed. Consider the following aspects, which have a significant impact on the size of the integration task:

▌ How much overlap is there between the customer base of the two companies?

▌ What variance is there in the commercial terms applicable to key common customers?

▌ What is the current market coverage of each company's sales team?

▌ What is the profitability of each company's product, per country and market segment?

▌ How much overlap is there between the two companies' portfolios: any duplicates?

▌ How are the product and customer hierarchies organised? What common format might be used in the future?

▋ What is the cost breakdown structure in manufacturing of the two companies? Which are the main options for the future manufacturing footprint?

▋ What are the current costs associated with each office and production location?

▋ What definitions can be used to rapidly build a database of the entire headcount of the two companies in order to have a common denomination for job descriptions, salary bands, hierarchy levels etc

▋ What differences exist between the remuneration and benefits offered by the two companies to their employees? i.e. salary bands, bonus schemes, appraisal systems, pension funds, etc.

One of the activities that is typically very time consuming is the formulation of common definitions and measurements – how to compare like with like across the two companies that are about to integrate. These definitions need to be in place before any data gathering exercise can begin, and they need to be rigorously thought through to ensure that all the relevant data can be collected in a single phase, thus avoiding the need to subsequently initiate several other data gathering exercises that will only serve to irritate the staff before the integration has even begun. Here again, the help of some experienced auditing or consulting firms can be invaluable, as they should be able to rapidly set up some data gathering templates that will lay out all the information required, ready for analysis.

Using the outputs of the initial analysis

The third party carrying out the analysis will not be allowed to release any of the details of the analysis until the two companies are jointly owned, but at that point the integration process will have saved several months compared with a 'cold start'. This will also be the right time to agree what market research data may be required so that the information gathered prior to Day One can be considered within the context of the broader market. In addition to having a better understanding of the areas that will present particular challenges during the integration, knowing what information will be available from Day One and in what format it will be accessible allows many of the decision tools to be prepared in advance.

The decision tools to establish what criteria will be used to select the future locations of the integrated company's offices, how products in the portfolio will be prioritised, how the market coverage and customer call frequency will be established, how the organisation design of the sales force will be optimised relative to that customer coverage, and so on. This is absolutely crucial for large scale international integrations, because similar decisions will need to be made in several countries or divisions of the company, and agreeing the *criteria* that will govern those decisions is necessary to prevent ad hoc choices which will undermine the coherence of the future organisation and the efficiency of its processes.

Setting up the project team

Creating the project's environment

A lot needs to be done before the bulk of the members of the project team can start working: deciding what tools and software suites will be used, establishing how the project will be planned and monitored, nominating the members of the project's board (Steering Committee), finding some office space and meeting rooms to accommodate the project team, and setting up a data repository where all the documents relating to the integration project will be stored. In many cases, it will not be possible to co-locate all the members of the project team, either because of geographical distance, or because there is no suitable space available in the companies' offices to accommodate the whole team. This no longer matters nowadays are there are excellent means of sharing information in virtual teams that no longer require the physical proximity that was so essential until the mid 1990s.

Here again, it will be necessary to remember to allow some time to set up this environment, establish the filing structure for the documents that will be held on this common platform, decide which access rights will be given to each of the project's work streams or to individual team members, and devise some form of induction training so that the entire project team can begin using the document repository.

Having the document repository up and running in time for the project team members to start using it from their first day on the project will prevent multiple versions of the same document being used simultaneously on several members' computers, and thus ensures that everyone has access to the same most recent version of any document.

In most companies, people are used to sharing documents on their company's intranet, or by accessing 'shared drives'. Even if this can be done across companies by establishing links between their respective networks, remember that this cannot be done between two merging companies until they have a common owner and are officially freed from all the competition clauses imposed by the regulatory authorities. Consequently, the shared document repository will need to be set up on a third-party's platform. Some large consultancies or accountancy firms offer such web spaces to their customers; but it is also possible to subscribe to these services with specialised companies, which usually offer very flexible functionality. The latter is my preferred solution because it allows the merging companies to continue using that shared document repository as long as they wish, even after the consultants and other advisors have left. Furthermore, if several firms of consultants and advisors are involved in supporting the integration project, giving access to one consultancy's proprietary website to consultants from other firms might prove problematic. Using an independent third-party's document repository gives the merging companies complete freedom to decide, user by user, who can access what document and how long the document repository will remain in use.

Over time, most companies will want the entire content of the external document repository to be transferred to their own systems and intranet, but there is at least no time pressure to get this done when an independent third party repository is being used. This gives the IT team the ability to focus on more urgent tasks, such as the integration of the companies' email systems, development of common data warehouses or the integration of the merged company's internet website to support the new corporate identity.

A number of platforms to share documents in a secure way across project teams available on the Internet. One of the best known is SharePoint® but new platforms emerge on the market all the time, and carrying out a web search on 'web-based collaboration and document management platform' or 'Web Collaboration Tool' should provide you with a comprehensive list of what is available and best suited to your requirements.

Initial training: establishing the team's common way of working

With a few exceptions, the people selected to join the project team will have been chosen on the basis of their knowledge of the business and their ability to think beyond the status quo to shape the future company, rather than on their mastery of project management techniques. Indeed, it is worth remembering that for many. if not most, of the project team members, this will be their first experience with any change programme of this magnitude. If properly handled, this is a fantastic learning experience, but on the one condition that the project's environment is well organised and prepared ahead of the integration's kick-off.

This means that prior to doing anything else on the project, the team members will need to undergo some form of induction. The induction will need to cover a number of aspects:

▌ **House rules**: everything that applies to the general administration and ways of working of the project, including how the team members are expected to claim their expenses related to the project, travel and hotel accommodation guidelines, organisation chart of 'who is who' on the project,

93

contact list, addresses of offices, working hours, dress code… all the things the team members knew about their respective companies, but which might be different now that individuals from two different companies need to operate as one homogenous team.

■ **Legal requirements**: a clear briefing regarding what information can be shared prior to Day One, and rules governing the confidentiality of sensitive information throughout the duration of the project. Most companies require team members to sign a confidentiality document. This is particularly important as some members of the integration team will, in the course of their project work, be exposed to data to which they would not normally have access, particularly data relating to internal costs that are needed to compare the relative merits of alternative scenarios, or confidential strategic projects that may impact the area of the business on which they are working. The briefing must also raise awareness on the severe consequences that would result from any breach of the rules and the magnitude of the fines that are imposed on companies in such circumstances. The aim here is to ensure that all members of the project team understand the importance of adhering very strictly to the 'firewall' rules that apply until the two companies have a common owner, and to handling sensitive information with the appropriate level of care.

■ **Project management basics:** induction into how the project plans will be structured to ensure that all the work streams plan to a similar degree of detail, and that they all use a common terminology that will then allow the various work stream plans to be consolidated into one overall master plan. Definition of key milestones and how these will be tracked. Project organisation and governance. Reporting procedures and process for issue reporting, escalation and resolution. Depending on how much experience the team members have of project work, particularly the individuals who are given the responsibility of leading a work stream, it may be necessary to take some people through an induction course on project planning, and particularly the process of planning *backwards*, from the end deliverables of a project back to the sub-components of those deliverables and the actions required to produce each of these. This is important because many individuals find it difficult, when developing a project plan, to translate a conceptual objective - such as 'integrating the product range' - into a set of tangible deliverables that together produce that outcome, and then break down those deliverables into sequences of specific action steps. Until they are familiarised with that process, they will not be capable of producing a solid project plan.

■ **Use of system tools**: ensure all the project team members have sufficient computer skills to work efficiently with spreadsheets and presentation software, as well as project planning software if a suite such as Microsoft Project® is being used. In many instances it may be possible to write up and manage the project plans using a spreadsheet software such as Microsoft Excel® with which most members of the team will be familiar, thus avoiding the need for a broad-scale induction into Microsoft Project® or similar tools that offer very advanced functionality but are best used by seasoned project managers and experienced project management office support staff.

■ **Document repository and document filing structure**: it is imperative that the filing structure of the abundant documentation that will be generated during the course of the integration project be defined from the onset, so that team members do not subsequently lose precious time seeking information that was created or updated by other members of the team. Everyone needs to be clear on the naming conventions that will apply to all documents generated by the team, where these need to be stored and who has authorised access to what type of document, either in 'read-only' mode, or as fully authorised creators and editors of documents.

■ **Risk Management basics**: the aspiration here is not to turn the project team members into specialist in risk management, but rather to give them an overview of how risks will be identified, monitored and managed, and clarify accountabilities in developing contingency plans and 'owning' risks.

■ **Stakeholder Management basics**: a quick overview of how stakeholders will be defined, categorised and managed, to build an awareness among the project team members of the importance of good stakeholder management in driving change through the organisation.

■ **Values:** a statement and articulation of the future company's values. This will help the members of the project team better understand what the target organisation will feel like, and act from the onset of the project as a microcosm of that future environment, which others across the organisation will emulate over time. In addition, getting clarity and alignment on company values can play a significant role in building team cohesion (see Chapter 8: "Team Cohesion: togetherness and common purpose")

As further individuals will join the project team over the duration of the integration, it can be worth investing some time and effort into pulling the above information into a small binder that can be given to each member of the integration team as a sort of 'starter kit' or be stored in electronic format on the project's intranet space, as this will avoid the need for repeated induction workshops and thus speed up the introduction of future newcomers to the team. This written documentation also promotes greater compliance with the house rules applicable to the team throughout the duration of the integration project.

Designing large scale multi-site business integrations

Addressing market diversity

When the integration of two companies only includes a limited number of sites or subsidiaries, it remains possible for the various work streams of the project to cover the scope of the entire organisation and deal with the specificities of each pair of businesses that need to be integrated two by two. This is no longer the case when the integration process spans a large number of business units that are geographically dispersed. One single integration team will not be able to resolve the multiplicity of issues and tailor-made solutions that are required to accommodate the diversity that can be found in such large organisations.

The word 'diversity' is key here. Any company working across geographies will be aware of the number of market-specific parameters that shape the environment in which they operate, whether these result from the company's competitive strength or history in a particular market, or from external factors beyond its control, such as employment legislation, distribution channels, transportation networks, trade regulations, consumption trends etc. And yet, in spite of these obvious differences, many companies embarking on an international integration are tempted to build a generic blue-print model of what two merged subsidiaries would look like, run a pilot in one market to fine-tune the model, and then expect to roll it out to all the other markets. It should come as no surprise that this 'one size fits all' approach is unlikely to succeed, primarily because one or several aspects of the proposed model will be inapplicable in each market, and secondly also because even if the company operates a business model that is well suited to international standardisation, the lack of involvement of local teams during the roll-out is likely to generate resistance to change.

The other extreme, which would be to devolve all decisions relating to the integration to the local in-market business units, will not work either. Mergers and major acquisitions are a perfect opportunity to improve a business and to roll-out processes that will enable the newly formed enlarged organisation to work efficiently and seamlessly across functional and geographical borders. However, this can only be achieved through a very tightly controlled coordination of the integration across all of the impacted business units. Rather than attempting to roll out the blueprint of the 'ideal in-market subsidiary', what needs to be common across all of the business units is the *decision criteria*, the factors that will be taken into consideration to design each of the newly-merged business units, not the design itself.

Mandating the 'how', not the 'what'

Because the same decisions will need to be made almost simultaneously in a number of business units in large merging organisations, it is imperative to give each of the teams in charge of those integration projects very clear guide-lines as to how they are expected to analyse their market and business variables, and the criteria according to which they will design the end-state of their integration. One of the key reasons for doing this, in addition to avoiding the need for each of the local integration teams to re-invent the wheel, is to ensure coherence in the integration process across the entire organisation and to allow comparisons to be made between the business units in spite of the inherent differences that exist between the markets in which they operate. This is important because in the absence of such criteria of comparison, it would not be possible for the organisation to optimise the allocation of resources between its constituent businesses.

To illustrate this, let us take Sales Organisation Design as an example. The number of sales people required to cover a territory is dependent among other factors on the number of customers and the frequency of sales calls. But according to what criteria will one decide how broad a customer coverage is warranted on a market, or how frequently a customer should be visited. Is it customer profitability? Customer potential? Customer type? Customer location? The range of products bought by that customer?

It is most probably a combination of all of the above, but unless all of the integration teams base their decision on a common scorecard that describes how each of these variables must be considered, what weighting each one carries in the overall scoring scale, and defines a common breakdown of customer types, it will be impossible to compare the organisation designs proposed by the various businesses. And yet this is essential as only through such like-with-like comparisons can the investment in sales resources be optimised across the markets. How else can one decide whether the company would benefit from having fewer salesmen in, say, the Netherlands and more in Greece?

Likewise, planning the integration and rationalisation of the product portfolio requires similar criteria to be used across all markets. This assumes the use of similar tools to model the market, categorise consumers, and assess product profitability and potential. The outcome of such an analysis will differ widely from one market to another, because profitability levels are likely to vary, and the relative competitive strength of each product will be different from one market to another. A product that is the market leader in one country might be relatively unknown in another, and so the overall portfolio of products can, using the same method of analysis method, be remarkably different in one country compared to another. Here again, however, because the same methodology will have been used by every country to select and prioritise the products of the integrated range, the allocation of manufacturing capacity, marketing funds and other limited resources between the various products and countries can take place in a rational manner, based on a coherent set of decision criteria.

Each of the decisions requiring a complex set of inputs and evaluation criteria needs to be formalised in a clearly documented methodology that can be explained to the integration teams and which then allows them then to carry out the implementation with a fair degree of autonomy.

Developing and documenting these decision tools is a very time-consuming task, but the big advantage is that this can be done, or at least started and partly completed, well before Day One. Large international mergers or acquisitions are in most cases subject to a lengthy approval process by trade regulatory authorities, but this time can be put to good use in preparing the decision tools. In doing this, a team responsible for developing one such methodology can evaluate various approaches and select the most appropriate one without the strong time pressure that would prevail if this were done during the project's implementation phase.

Another benefit that the development of standardised decision tools offers during large scale integrations is that the central integration team, which will have the task of reviewing project plans and progress with each of the regional or country integration teams, will be able to focus these reviews on the outcome of the decisions and proposals made by each of those teams, rather than debating how they reached those conclusions. This saves a lot of valuable time for everyone, and avoids struggles or power games between 'The Centre' and the various operating business units.

The tool kit

Preparing a comprehensive set of tools for the markets to use during their integration will take several months, typically anything between two and six months depending on the desired degree of detail. Much of this can take place before Day One because all that is required at this stage is agreement between the two merging companies about *how* the decisions would be made, not what those decisions will be. Consequently, no exchange of sensitive data is needed to progress this work and this is therefore fully compliant with the rules set by the regulatory authorities.

Broadly, a comprehensive tool kit would comprise the following sections:

- **Communications**: a set of core messages, or even generic presentation slides, which can tailed and used by the markets in staff briefings after Day One.

- **General principles**: this is a set of rules that will govern decision-making during the integration process, and are basically a high-level summary of the key points arising from the tool-kit's modules. For example, what principles will govern the staff selection, what are the main steps that will shape the future integrated product portfolio, and so on. This allows each of the integration work streams to have a broad understanding of what the other teams will be addressing during the integration process, before delving into the detail of the tasks their own work stream will need to tackle. Additionally, the general principles can be integrated into the internal communications because they will be a good means of reassuring the staff about the integration process, proving that it has been rigorously thought through and planned, and that the company is not about to live through a troubled period of internal lobbying and power games.

▌ **Organisation of the integration programme**: overall governance of the programme, progress review process, calendar of key meetings or reporting dates, key milestones, generic integration plan, as well as guide-lines on how to select, organise, manage and re-deploy in-market integration teams.

▌ **Data templates**: as explained earlier, a lot of the data that will be required during the integration process can be gathered, separately, by each of the merging companies. Therefore, some of the data templates will need to be released well in advance of Day One to start the data collation as soon as possible. But further templates may be included in the tool-kit to explain how the separate sets of data emanating from the two organisations need to be compared, analysed or consolidated after Day One.

▌ **Decision tools**: these are the modules that will apply to the various work streams, assuming the teams have been organised by 'outcome' rather than by functional department. Inevitably this will be the most important section, volume wise, and covers topics such as organisation design, route to market, portfolio integration, selection of office locations, integration of IT systems, integration of commercial terms and conditions, HR policies and benefits, supply chain integration, manufacturing footprint integration, etc.

101

Including a skeleton implementation plan that the market teams can tailor to their needs saves time compared to having each market starting off with a blank sheet, and serves as a very useful checklist for these teams who otherwise may not think of a number of steps that need to be considered during the course of their integration. Additionally, asking all of the markets to base themselves on that project plan will make life easier for the central programme management office in charge of supervising and coordinating the markets' integration efforts as all of the plans will have a similar outline structure with only a few country specific sections.

> *All that is required at this stage is agreement between the two merging companies about how the decisions would be made, not what those decisions will be.*

Fine tuning before large scale implementation

In theory, the toolkit that will have been pulled together during the months running up to Day One will comprise almost everything the country teams need to successfully carry out their integration. In practice, even if the toolkit is comprehensive, it may be that some elements of it may be difficult for the country teams to understand or execute, while others may be beyond the capability and experience of the project team and require additional support and coaching. This may turn out to be a major issue if a large number of markets are involved in the integration, as the central team will not have the means to assist each market on those complex or challenging topics.

Before rolling-out the integration methodology to all the markets in a large company, it is wise to run a short pilot with an average sized market. To save time, this can also take place with dummy data and therefore be scheduled before Day One. Alternatively, the pilot will need to be scheduled to take place during the very first weeks after Day One so that any adjustments to the toolkit that might be required can be developed rapidly and the rest of the markets can kick-off their own integration as soon as possible.

Kick-off

A clearly structured and well-documented took-kit, perfected with the learning derived from the pilot, provides the base for an efficient induction of all the integration project teams. These can then be brought together, regionally, and taken through the general sections of the took-kit as well as the specific modules relating to their particular function and work stream.

In large organisations, the number of people involved in the integration process will not allow all the work stream members to be gathered in one venue during one same week. If the project is about the 'integration of equals', the number of participants attending the initial kick-off event can rapidly develop to quite a crowd, considering that the delegation from each business unit would typically include its Managing Director, as well as the heads of Finance, Sales, Marketing, Human Resources, Information Systems, Logistics, and Manufacturing i.e. up to seven delegates per company, times two as each market will comprise two companies, since two companies are about to integrate. As a result, the list of attendees for the initial induction will need to be limited to those members of the Executive teams from both organisations in each market, who will then have the responsibility of running their own 'kick-off' and induction sessions in their respective markets. Here again, the documented tool-kit will ensure that this is done in a uniform way across geographies.

Getting these executives under one roof to kick-off the integration programme is a good opportunity for them to meet their counterparts from the other company, and be made aware of their key responsibilities in driving the integration process to a successful outcome in their respective markets. The logistics of such a kick-off event can be complex and need to be planned carefully, since there may be up to 14 delegates per market, in addition to the members of the central team who are running the induction sessions. Some of the modules of the induction will be run as plenary sessions, others in small functional teams or cross-functional teams, and finally some round-up modules will be run in country teams, particularly towards the end of the induction as this will be the opportunity for each country team to agree on its action plan before returning to their market to brief their respective teams.

Depending on the complexity and number of modules that need to be presented, the initial induction workshop can last three or four days which, together with travel, wipes out an entire week from the executives' calendar shortly after Day One. However, the time invested in thoroughly developing the tool-kit, making the Executive teams fully aware of their role and responsibility for the success of the integration, and running the induction programme to ensure they all understand the content of the modules and can train their own teams, will be a significant accelerator from that point onwards, shortening by several months the time needed by each of the markets to integrate.

In large companies comprising a number of national subsidiaries, or other such business units, by the time the integration kick-off briefings take place the general managers of those business units might have already been appointed. If this is the case, it will be necessary before the kick-off event to carefully consider what the expected role of the non-appointed individuals will be. Particularly in integrations that aim to be a 'merger of equals', it can be helpful to include both the appointed general manager of each business unit as well as the individual who did *not* get that job, to prevent that person's team from seeing themselves as the losers, the 'orphans', the 'victims' of a take-over.

The so-called 'non-appointed general manager' can bring considerable market and sector knowledge to the integration process, and can play a constructive role in reassuring his or her team that the rules of 'fair-play' will be applied throughout the integration. The extent to which this is feasible will depend very much on the temperament of the non-appointed general managers: some of them will be professional to the very last day and fulfil this difficult role to the best of their ability in exchange for a handsome redundancy package or simply as a result of their own high standards of business ethics. In other cases, I have seen some non-appointed general managers behave like helpless victims and seriously undermine the morale and cohesion of their integration team. If this happens, it will probably be best to forego the opportunity of capturing that uncooperative person's knowledge and remove him or her from the integration as soon as possible, to avoid a noxious impact on the rest of the team.

Suggested high-level structure of an integration kick-off event

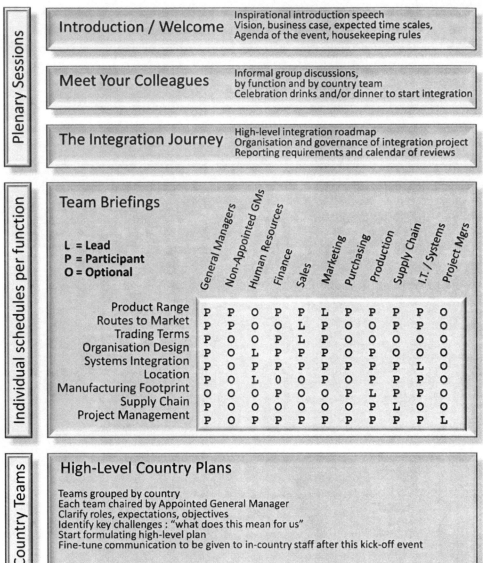

Plenary Sessions

Introduction / Welcome
Inspirational introduction speech
Vision, business case, expected time scales,
Agenda of the event, housekeeping rules

Meet Your Colleagues
Informal group discussions,
by function and by country team
Celebration drinks and/or dinner to start integration

The Integration Journey
High-level integration roadmap
Organisation and governance of integration project
Reporting requirements and calendar of reviews

Individual schedules per function

Team Briefings

L = Lead
P = Participant
O = Optional

	General Managers	Non-Appointed GMs	Human Resources	Finance	Sales	Marketing	Purchasing	Production	Supply Chain	I.T. / Systems	Project Mgrs
Product Range	P	P	O	P	P	L	P	P	P	P	O
Routes to Market	P	P	O	O	L	P	O	O	P	P	O
Trading Terms	P	O	O	P	L	P	O	O	O	O	O
Organisation Design	P	O	L	P	P	P	O	P	O	O	O
Systems Integration	P	O	P	P	P	P	P	P	P	L	O
Location	P	O	L	O	O	P	O	P	P	P	O
Manufacturing Footprint	O	O	O	P	O	O	P	L	P	P	O
Supply Chain	P	O	O	O	O	O	O	P	L	O	O
Project Management	P	O	P	P	P	P	P	P	P	P	L

Country Teams

High-Level Country Plans

Teams grouped by country
Each team chaired by Appointed General Manager
Clarify roles, expectations, objectives
Identify key challenges : "what does this mean for us"
Start formulating high-level plan
Fine-tune communication to be given to in-country staff after this kick-off event

In Essence...

■ *Thorough preparation is key to allow the integration process to hit the road running as soon as the two companies are under common ownership.*

■ *Get clarity from qualified legal counsel as to what information can be shared or not, and ensure that these rules are well understood and applied by all the people involved in the pre-integration preparation. Remember to continue operating as competitors until Day One.*

■ *Data analysis by a third party bound by a confidentiality agreement can 'pre-digest' the work by defining the tools and templates that will be used for the integration, and identifying areas of particular complexity, thus allowing the project team to be resourced accordingly.*

■ *Preparation should as a minimum attempt to establish common data definitions, so that all the data required for the integration can be gathered in standardised comparable formats ahead of Day One: this can be a very lengthy process, so the sooner it can commence, the better.*

■ *Set up the project environment in advance so that everything the team members need is available when they start working on the project.*

■ *In large organisations comprising numerous business units, focus the preparation on developing decisions tools: these will allow the business units to progress in their integration, in parallel, without constant input from 'the Centre'.*

■ *Pitch the kick-off event so that it is both informative and creates energy. Decide ahead of that date what role you wish non-appointed senior managers to have in the integration process.*

Due Diligence

You don't know what you don't know

Someone browsing through the index of this book might wonder why I chose to write about an integration's structure, organisation, planning and kick-off before addressing the topic of due diligence. My reason for doing so is that I wanted to give a clear sense of how much needs to happen before the integration process can even commence, and show how some of that preparation work as well as the integration itself can be greatly helped by probing a few areas in addition to those traditionally covered during due diligence.

The fact that so many companies believe there is little or no preparation they can carry out before completing the acquisition or merger transaction results in the entire focus being placed on the transaction itself, rather than on its consequence, namely the need for two organisations to then blend into one. "Are we paying the right price" is therefore the big question in the forefront of the Executive's thoughts. However, should the Executive be talking about the price being paid for the company in its present state, or its value as it will be when it will have been transformed and the integration is complete?

Looking at the journey rather than just the end destination

Typically, the armada of accountants, consultants and other specialists in charge of carrying out a due diligence exercise will focus on estimating the asset and economic value of the target company as it stands today, and evaluating the potential synergies that can be derived from combining the two businesses. In most cases, far less consideration is given to the factors that may give the integration teams and senior management sleepless nights during the journey that separates 'today' from the day when the two organisations will be seamlessly integrated.

My intention here is not to draw up an exhaustive list of items to be covered during due diligence, but rather highlight a few 'oft forgotten time bombs': elements that would not be an issue for the company in its present state, but which may result in greatly increasing the cost of the integration or extending its duration. Some of these have a clear impact on the price one *should* pay for the target company or, just as importantly, on the likelihood of really deriving the synergies and other benefits that were initially described and quantified in the merger or acquisition's business case, on time and in full.

By the same token, particularly in the case of acquisitions rather than mergers (as the latter assume a mutual willingness to integrate), a few helpful items can be negotiated and included in the acquisition agreement to lay the path for more efficient preparation and a smoother execution of the integration. These are discussed below.

Agreeing to cooperate

One of the first items to address is whether the company that is being acquired will accept to engage in early preparation work prior to Day One, within the limits of what is permissible under the legal restrictions set out by the regulators. Let us remind ourselves here that while the disclosure of any type of even slightly sensitive commercial information is prohibited by legislation until the two companies are under common ownership, agreeing on the approach that would be taken to integrate the two organisations and on the type of data that needs to be gathered to proceed with that work is admissible, as well as aligning on definitions that will allow the data to be compared and analysed on a like-with-like basis. Legal counsel should be sought on a case-by-case basis to avoid any breach of the applicable legislation.

We saw earlier that this preparation work ahead of the day the companies have a common owner can be invaluable, but the underlying assumption for this to happen is that both companies are willing to play the game. In a merger, both companies involved have a clear interest in ensuring everything runs smoothly in their common future. This is not as obvious when one company is acquired by the other. The acquired company will put its best endeavours to ensure that everything runs smoothly until the acquisition transaction is completed, and furthermore that nothing takes place during that time that could cause a future prejudice that would allow the acquirer to substantiate claims for compensation – but all of this does not amount to active collaboration in extracting data, adjusting the data to agreed template formats, and freeing up resources to start jointly planning the integration together with the team nominated by the acquirer.

Other reasons can prompt the acquired company to be very secretive until Day One, and one of the main reasons is that before being acquired, businesses are often eyed by several potential buyers, each of which will have conducted some form of due diligence, sometimes to a great degree of depth and thoroughness, and each of these is very demanding on the staff of the company that is up for sale. Once the winning bidder has been identified and detailed talks take place to draw up the legal documents and apply for regulatory approval, one can understand that the staff and management of the company that is about to be bought will welcome a break, having already answered a myriad of questions to accountants and consultants during the due diligence process, before embarking on the final data gathering exercise that will serve as the basis for the integration.

In one of the integrations I led, the CEO of the company that was being acquired refused any contact from taking place between members of the management of the two parties until Day One, thereby blocking any attempt by those teams to discuss what type of data needed to be gathered and how the integration would be organised to allow sufficient preparation work ahead of the integration kick-off. Instead, that CEO required that any discussions be channelled through one single member of his Executive team, which greatly slowed down the flow of communication and prevented it from reaching the level of detail that would have been required. He motivated his decision by a willingness to 'protect' his team and spare them the stress and worry of being confronted with people from the acquiring company. From the perspective of the acquiring company, this was highly frustrating because in addition to delaying the start date and the quality of the pre-merger planning, it prevented them from getting a first impression of the calibre of management that was present in the business they were buying.

Whatever the motives for refusing any orderly dialogue between the two companies that are about to integrate, we need to bear in mind that delaying the integration process by several months, and not allowing that integration to take place in as smooth a way as it potentially could, bears a price. This should be considered when negotiating the final details of the deal. In the case I mentioned above, the management of the acquired company had no obligation under the agreement to cooperate in the pre-planning process and gather information in standardised formats, as a result of which most of this work could only commence three months later once the acquisition transaction was completed.

Agreeing what and by whom

Being specific about what type of information will be gathered and analysed ahead of Day One will help avoid any stressful conversations and haggling in the run-up to the acquisition or merger transaction. It will therefore be necessary to have some formal agreement on which third-party will be authorised to access and compare sensitive information, and what must be done with the information thus gathered in the event that the acquisition or merger transaction does not ultimately take place – because there is always a slight risk that regulatory approval will not be given or that some other fundamental condition is not met.

The unknown clauses of employment contracts

This is another classic source of unwelcome surprises. The due diligence process will have gathered the organisation charts of the companies, but not necessarily had visibility of the employment contracts relating to the key players in the business. These may (and often do) contain special clauses regarding the contract's termination with expensive golden parachutes, or may include restrictive definitions of the incumbents' roles in the business, or specific reporting lines.

This can be a minefield as some of these clauses may seriously restrict the extent to which such individuals can be meaningfully re-deployed in the future company's integrated organisation. While such clauses end up, in practice, being included in contracts for the sole purpose of confirming the status of a particular position and therefore do not have a real impact on the daily running of a job, they can of course be invoked as motives for unilateral termination when significant changes are made in the organisation. In one of my recent projects, while the organisation chart of the acquired company looked fairly conventional, it turned out that whereas the CEO theoretically had six direct reports, a total of 19 people in the organisation had contracts stipulating that they report directly to the CEO. Several individuals who were subsequently offered senior positions in the new organisation that did *not* report directly to the CEO claimed this was a material deterioration in their employment terms, in spite of the fact that the enlarged size of the combined integrated company broadened the scope and magnitude of the new proposed job. Consequently, the company was forced to declare these individuals redundant, resulting in high compensation payouts.

The contractual definition of jobs can also be a significant constraint, particularly in highly regulated or unionised environments. This can greatly reduce the ability to make fundamental changes to the company's organisation design.

While it is, of course, not possible for two companies to read through each other's employee contracts prior to Day One, the above details could easily be checked by an external party and flagged as either potential constraints that will affect the integration, or risks in terms of integration costs. In both cases, these factors have a dilution impact on the value of the merger or acquisition's business case.

Social plans and precedents

A lot of time is usually devoted during a due diligence process to a detailed analysis of the other company's pension scheme, for very understandable reasons. And yet, the same level of attention is not always given to social plans and the study of specific cases of employment contract terminations of the past few years, systematically, across all the company's subsidiaries. In the absence of such information, the costs associated with changes in the organisation's design are likely to be under-estimated. Even if the details of a recent social plan are available, there may be cases where some individuals' particular circumstances will have resulted in greater severance payouts or other benefits than those resulting from the social plan, and these will be invoked when the organisations are being merged. So it makes sense to find out about these exceptions during the due diligence process rather than being faced with a bad surprise during the integration, with potentially significant unbudgeted costs.

Data completeness

Checking for data completeness and accuracy during the due diligence process can be immensely helpful, because this will determine how much preparation work can be carried out before Day One and, consequently, provide a better indication of how long the integration process is likely to last. By doing this, the company can set the right expectations from the onset when the first communications are made about the planned merger or acquisition.

Also, if some of the data is patchy or needs to be cleansed (which is very often the case), steps can be taken rapidly to ensure the resources are made available for that exercise. One area in particular that is worth checking is the completeness and accuracy of the data relating to the headcount and organisation design. Several integrations in which I was involved struggled with the reconciliation of data emanating from different sources: typically, medium sized or large organisations have more 'bodies' working in them than would be suggested by the payroll, because of the presence of contractors, temporary staff, consultants or people working for companies to which the organisation has outsourced some activities. Conversely, staff on maternity leave or long-term absence for sickness are found on the payroll data, but not on the organisation charts. There can be double or treble counting of individuals who work in several sites. Inconsistencies between the number of individuals, the number of 'full time equivalents' and number of 'bums on seats' add further complexity to the overall picture.

This information is essential to correctly assess the likely cost of any changes in organisation design that will take place during the integration process. In addition to this, nominal lists of staff are needed in negotiations with trade unions or works councils, and any gaps in information or inaccuracies are likely to be interpreted as a sign of contempt of senior management vis-à-vis the company's staff, which will cause resentment.

A quick final check by 'someone who knows'

The reason I have included a section on due diligence in this book is that many of the hurdles I encountered during the integrations in which I have been involved could easily have been avoided "if only we'd known", and the aim of a thorough due diligence should be precisely this: no surprises.

It is difficult, and probably quite risky, to make sweeping generalisations as to what additional information would be valuable in a due diligence relating to a company that needs to undergo an integration, as opposed to a mere acquisition of a company that is destined to remain a stand-alone unit. Much of this will depend on the type of company, the industry in which it operates, and other such specific circumstances. The topics I have listed above are information gaps that seem to be quite systematic, but the best way of getting a more industry-specific opinion during the final stages of the due diligence would be to involve someone who has ample experience of company integrations, to make sure that the findings will focus on the likely complexity of the integration process as well as on the company's valuation.

In the same way that most company integrations begin only after Day One and regrettably miss the fantastic opportunity to plan and prepare carefully in advance, even fewer companies think of seeking the views of someone who has 'been there/done that' before signing the documents that will lead to the acquisition or merger. And this is why I have repeatedly been exposed to the consequences of these missed opportunities. In a multi-site or international integration, the consequences of overlooking an important point during the due diligence process can be multiplied by the number of sites that will need integrating. These do not automatically lead to the failure of an integration project, but are guaranteed to cause a great deal of frustration, drag out the duration of the integration process, increase the implementation costs, and most probably fail to produce an optimised outcome, thus under-delivering the benefits that could potentially have been generated by the merger or acquisition.

In Essence...

▋ *In addition to assessing the value of a company in its present state, due diligence ahead of a business integration must consider those aspects that do not hinder the company's current daily business but may cause additional complexity or costs during the integration.*

▋ *The key factors that might slow down the integration process are poor quality or incomplete data, unwillingness to cooperate in the preparation work prior to Day One, lack of clarity as to what the preparation work will include and who is responsible for what piece of that work.*

▋ *Check for precedents in the company's last five to eight years: social plans, 'golden parachutes', exceptional terms applied to staff who either left the company or were transferred to other roles.*

▋ *High restructuring costs and legal issues may arise during the integration if there are significant discrepancies between senior employees' contractual terms and the reality of their actual role in the current organisation.*

Identity and Culture

Towards being One Whole, rather than Two Halves

Us and them

In aiming for the successful integration of two organisations, one of the rather intangible but nonetheless absolutely essential duties of the Executive and senior management is to define the future company's identity and culture, which will act as the 'cement' of the new organisation. This is what will bind individuals from different backgrounds and origins. The notion of 'identity and culture' would typically include a company's purpose, values, beliefs, philosophies, policies, and standards, as well as its brand or brands, all of which become its personality towards the outside world.

This is indeed a huge task, not least because it will cause a lot of debate as there is no single best solution and therefore much depends here on personal choices, and one that will then need to be 'sold' to the rest of the organisation. Even though some consultancies specialise in helping organisations formulate their identity, their support will mainly ensure that the end result is coherent and defendable, whereas the values and standards encapsulated in the newly-defined identity and culture will very much reflect those of the members of the top management team.

As a consequence of this, even if some top-line bullet points of the future company culture can be communicated on Day One, it will necessarily take some time for these headlines to be articulated and worded in a way that makes them come to life in the minds of the company's staff; particularly in the case of international companies. And therefore the issue that needs addressing in the very short term is to know what can be done to help people from both 'sides' start behaving like one team.

I have found that one of the simplest is to immediately stop using the words *us* and *them*, or *we* and *you*. It sounds so easy, and yet this does require a fair degree of vigilance to prevent this 'us and them' from slipping into conversations when integration team members are identifying differences between the two former companies and defining how the future business will operate: "*we* used to do it this way, how did *you* do it"? If Best Ltd. and Biggest Ltd. are merging, there is a clear advantage in saying "Best did it this way; how did Biggest do it?" because by formulating the phrase in that way, the people involved in the conversation are viewing their former companies from the outside, as individuals who have left their previous organisations and are now sharing a new environment together. Referring to the former companies by their name rather than 'us' and 'them' helps turn the page on the past. Best Inc. is no longer 'us', it might be 'what we used to be', and creating that break from the past can do a lot in focusing the minds forwards rather than building some kind of nostalgia about the way things used to be. Importantly, it avoids making repeated reference to the fact that there are two sides, two camps, and instead puts the emphasis on the need to establish common ways of working for everyone, regardless of the 'side' from which they originated.

As with many things, the example must come from the top, and therefore the Executive and leadership team members must make a conscious effort during the first weeks to avoid the use of terms that would crystallise the divide between the two former teams. This also means that the avoidance of *us* and *them* needs to feature clearly in all communication guide-lines, so that all the people responsible for cascading information through the company are aware of the reasons behind this choice and do not perceive it as purely semantic.

> *Referring to the former companies by their name rather than 'us' and 'them' helps turn the page on the past, focusing the minds forwards rather than building some kind of nostalgia about the way things used to be.*

Blend the ingredients

Getting individuals from the two former organisations to mix as early as possible is key, as this avoids the emergence of a pattern whereby people continue to gather in their former groupings of peers. Forcing this mix at the integration's kick-off meeting gives a strong signal. In most cases, it will be necessary to define a seating plan, not only at the tables if the meeting involves a meal, but also in the workshop rooms, as the delegates will otherwise tend to cluster with their colleagues, with the people they know – because these are the people who will make them feel safer in the uncomfortable circumstances of organisational change. Requiring individuals to quit their comfort zone and mix with strangers will feel awkward for most of them, and it is worth setting the record straight by explaining to them that this is a deliberate choice.

Building a new organisation based on the best of both constituent companies requires that everyone understands how the other company operated in the past, and therefore all the people in the room need to reach out to their respective counterparts. Beyond the members of the integration project's work streams, organising information sessions attended by a cross-section of staff from both companies is an effective way of extending this 'mix of ingredients' broadly across the organisation. This gives the attendees an opportunity to get to know each other and learn about the key strengths and heritage each of the companies is bringing to the future organisation. The faster the initial feelings of *fear of the unknown* can be replaced by *curiosity for the unknown*, the better. In the case of an acquisition, as opposed to a merger of equals, organising gatherings with mixed audiences from both the acquiring and acquired company is a powerful means – if this is what the Executive wants – of communicating that everyone, not only the acquired team, is now working for a new organisation.

> *The faster the initial feelings of **fear of the unknown** can be replaced by **curiosity for the unknown**, the better.*

Other visible signs of 'us and them'

In order to allow individuals from both companies to meet and mix effectively and seamlessly, some of the outward signs of belonging to either group need to be harmonised rapidly, if not people will be instantly identifiable as belonging to one particular group and the efforts to blend and mix will be made harder. This applies to many little details that some might consider to be trivial, but because they are visible to others and can be considered as part of the norms that define one's belonging to a group, they are worth considering here. One such detail is dress code. It would indeed be difficult to simulate being 'one team' when half the participants are dressed in formal business wear and the others turn up in open-collar sport shirts. Likewise, the degree of formality used by people from either company when addressing each other can be a distinctive outward sign of a divide between the two former cultures. Although being on first-name terms is often the norm in Anglo-Saxon cultures, the more formal Mr X and Mrs Y is still commonplace in many other cultures. Will the senior person opening a meeting refer to his or her counterpart in the other organisation by first name, or in a more formal way? How will the attendees feel comfortable introducing themselves and addressing their counterparts?

Other issues relating to formality may take longer to resolve, as some of these do not lend themselves to being easily mandated from the onset. For example, in languages that use a polite and familiar form, such as the "tu" and "vous" in French, or "du" and "Sie" in German, forcing everyone to use the informal form before they feel ready to do so may transgress a slight taboo.

In the longer run, one other crass detail that many companies omit to standardise across the whole organisation is job titles. Changing people's job titles can be a delicate matter, and indeed many companies will avoid confronting this issue by arguing quite rightly that it is the job description that really matters, not the wording of the job title. And yet different job titles for similar jobs effectively perpetuate an artificial divide that contradict the organisation's aim to integrate. They are a constant reminder of the past, which distracts people from looking forward towards a common future.

From "us and them" to "we": creating the new environment

Branding and symbols

Deploying the best efforts to create an environment in which the people from two companies can begin experiencing a feeling of common belonging goes a long way in alleviating fears and resistance to change, and it is therefore not surprising that many companies go what some might think is 'over the top' to promote this feeling of togetherness, of being part of 'one team'. Big numbers can be involved, particularly when it comes to re-modelling the company's headquarters and flanking the launch of the new corporate identity with a number of special events and branded giveaways to the staff. Viewed within the context of the overall cost of a merger, however, the investment required for the deployment of branding and symbols is money well spent as it plays such an important role in supporting the smooth integration of two communities.

Rolling out a common corporate brand identity and other visible manifestations of common belonging plays to one of our most basic instincts, which is to define group identity by the uniformity of perceptible signals. Just in the same way as nations choose to adopt a new flag after a regime change to mark a new beginning, rapidly rolling out a new logo, new stationery, new signage, new factory clothing or new uniforms where appropriate, and new business cards are a means of signalling the beginning of a new era, therefore implicitly closing the book on the past and helping the two communities of the constituent companies to join their efforts for a new common future.

Balance: the best of both

Many people believe that the need for a balanced approach, which attempts to capture and retain the best of what the two constituent companies had in terms of know-how and working practices, is only a key consideration in mergers, as opposed to acquisitions. Indeed some actually relish the somewhat conquering dynamics of a take-over, but this is likely to maintain a split between the two communities: winners and losers. There may well be, of course, instances where the sole purpose of an acquisition is to gain market share or geographical coverage rather than transform the fabric of a company, particularly when the acquisition only represents a relatively small add-on to an existing business. But on the other hand, if the acquisition represents a significant step forward for the acquiring company, or provides it with access to new technology or new ways of working, acknowledging this when designing the company's future environment will help prevent the emergence of two rival communities: the conquerors and the conquered. It can do much to avoid losing the specific attributes that made the acquired company attractive, as would happen if the conquerors were left free to replicate their ways of working in the company they are 'colonising'.

I witnessed an example of one such strong signal being sent across an organisation in an integration I recently led when the divisional headquarters of the acquiring company changed address to move abroad into the offices of the company they had just bought, thereby spelling out quite clearly that the new acquisition was not just a mere add-on of secondary importance.

In many cases, however, the circumstances or strategic priorities are such that one cannot project that ideal sense of balance when integrating the companies and the perception that the organisation breaks down into two groups – the conquerors and the conquered – will be hard to avoid. This does not prevent the integration from seeking to build on the best of both companies and to communicate this appropriately: it is a way of reassuring everyone that the heritage and know-out of the company that has been acquired will not go to waste.

In Essence...

▌ *Stop using 'us' and 'them' or 'you' and 'we'. Call the former companies by their name, without identifying with either to the detriment of the other.*

▌ *Identity and business culture must be 'lived', not just described: the example can only come from the top.*

▌ *Provide as many opportunities as possible for people from both business communities to mix. Force them to actually 'mix' rather than just attend one same event side by side.*

▌ *Do not underestimate the power of symbols: use the new corporate identity as a banner, in the same way as the flag of a new country.*

Leadership Style and Motivation

Has everything not already been written?

Unusual circumstances

There must be enough business literature on Leadership and Motivation to fill entire libraries. My purpose here is not to serve a re-baked version of what other authors have already said innumerable times, but rather to try to pinpoint from a more pragmatic stance what is different about leadership during a business integration, and also to list a few attributes that have proved to be effective in my experience thus far.

In normal times of 'business as usual', a company's leader(s) must paint a clear vision, sketch out the path that will lead to it, and generate some enthusiasm, energy and cohesion within the organisation so that individuals feel incited to do everything that will contribute towards progressing on the path to that vision. What is then so different during an integration process? The simple answer is that while ambitious companies are used to working at an intensive pace during normal times, things can become rather extreme during an integration because many individuals will be worried about their future, and therefore become less focused and less effective, just when the integration work is causing a huge overlay of work on top of the company's usual level of activity.

Whether the key players in the organisation and the members of the integration team have the energy, motivation and stamina to carry out the task to the end, or whether they will feel driven to exhaustion and finally snap, will very much depend on the Leadership from the very top of the organisation.

There are, of course, many different styles of effective leadership, suited to a variety of company cultures and environments. Rather than taking the risk of painting some kind of generic style of leadership that would suit all types of integration environments, I feel it wiser to look at the topic through the eyes of those who will be led, and understand why they might be in need of stronger leadership during their company's merger process.

The gym routine that hurts the muscles

Individuals are being asked to stretch beyond their own limits, not just once, but repeatedly during the integration phase, which can last many months, one year or even a little longer. Compare this with someone embarking on a routine of physical exercise at the local gym. Working in a 'business as usual' environment can be compared to someone performing a cardio-vascular routine and sweating it out on a treadmill or rowing machine, whereas implementing the integration of two complex organisations is probably closer to weight-lifting, stomach crunches or other such muscle-strengthening exercise.

On a treadmill, one gets into the rhythm of things: this requires self-discipline, persistence, consistency and energy not to stop half-way, but the exercise itself becomes a routine that can leave enough mental space to drift into other activities: many people running on the treadmill at their local gym watch TV to pass the time while they are running, and they have learned to perform their physical exercise routine without supervision or coaching.

But what if the regular 20 or 30 minute jogging routine on the treadmill is replaced by training for a full-length marathon? Observe people undergoing a form of physical training that either requires them to perform new movements or to surpass their limits and not to stop when the muscles really begin to ache, and many of them will either have a personal coach or will join a class led by a very vocal instructor. In the absence of that instructor, or without the pressure of the rest of the group performing those same painful exercises, there is a fair chance that most individuals would not carry out the programme of exercises to its full extent. Think of the skipper in a rowing race, shouting at the rowers to continue rowing, more, more, more, faster... Not only do the encouragements and energy of the skipper impregnate the rowers, but each of the rowers will perform to the outer limits of what can be endured to avoid letting the rest of the team down.

Likewise during the integration of two organisations, team dynamics play an important role because one wants to have built a strong cohesion within the team in order to reach the point where everyone keeps up the effort through mere consideration and solidarity with the other members of the team. But above all it is the charisma of the team leader(s) that will create the energy the team will need to withstand the prolonged work pressure of the integration programme. And while it is fair to say that the leadership skills and style required to drive the integration of two companies are not markedly different compared to those applied to normal 'business as usual', the leader's ability is certainly put to the test by the extreme conditions of the integration environment.

Team cohesion: togetherness and common purpose

Building a strong sense of cohesion in the integration team requires some time and effort. Unlike a functional team, in which people have probably followed similar studies, share common knowledge and may have followed similar career paths, the integration team by definition spans most or all of the company's functions. This is a group of people who, apart from having the shared objective of defining the ways of integrating two businesses and then implementing that plan, would otherwise probably not be attracted to each other for lack of commonality. Indeed, owing to the transient nature of an integration team, it is unlikely that individuals would strongly seek to bond with each other when their main concern, certainly during the early days of the project, will be to know how and when they will be able to re-connect with their former colleagues in their functional team when the integration is completed.

The creation of a 'bubble' that embraces the entire team and provides its members with a sense of common belonging is a crucial responsibility of the company's senior leadership. As for the rowers in the boat race, creating an environment in which the team members can bond is essential: this is what will give the team members the degree of commitment and dedication to meet deadlines and cope with their inordinate workload and travel schedule.

The added benefit of creating a strong sense of cohesion in the team is that it significantly enhances the perception that the individuals in that team will retain of the project when it has ended. And whereas we know that people usually tend to shy away from project work, those who have positive memories of the experience are likely to comment favourably about it across the company. They are more likely to offer themselves voluntarily as candidates for the company's next big project, or certainly make it easier for the company to recruit other individuals to join the team of that next project. Sharing a challenging experience can create strong bonds between people – we know this from our days in university, where small teams working long hours in the run-up to year-end exams often remain good friends for decades or a whole lifetime. Likewise in the campus-like life that can surround a large-scale integration project.

Getting the team members to socialise and create a bond and sustaining it

Remember that the individuals selected to join the integration team were chosen for their knowledge, but also for their ability to envisage ways of doing things differently. They will tend to be inquisitive and curious by nature. This is helpful as it will incite them to engage spontaneously in dialogue with the other members of their new team to find out what makes them tick, understand their opinions, express their own, etc.

In most cases, project teams of any significant size will comprise one or two 'live wires', the self-proclaimed organisers of social activities, and this is an excellent thing because such individuals have the ability to relieve the senior leadership of the responsibility for setting up the activities that will continue to fuel the sense of common identity in the team. But this will take time to emerge, and as the team was only set up for the medium term, generating the cement that will hold the team together in time for when the work pace intensifies requires immediate action in the very early stages of the project.

Some consultants claim to be specialists in team building, and get groups of people to perform activities and experience metaphors of daily life to improve their understanding of their own behaviours and those of others around them. This works well for some people, and less for others, particularly in cultures or business environments in which people do not feel comfortable with the concepts of metaphors, role-play or cathartic group discussions. Given that companies that are in the process of merging are usually swamped by consultants from every walk of life, the management of people and the creation of an environment that is both embracing and motivating is a responsibility, which, in my opinion, senior management should take on personally rather than delegating it to external consultants.

It is true that once the company has reached a certain degree of stability after the integration there may well be a need for facilitated sessions across the entire business: these can address dysfunctional areas or teams within the organisation, hone in on the possible behavioural causes of these problems and thereby define the path to resolve them. In the context of the early stages of integration, however, the environment is much more fluid and the target culture of the future company is not yet established, and it is therefore best for the members of the team to remain flexible, and be open to each other in the way that comes most naturally to them through socialising rather than through normative team exercises.

So what type of social activities can achieve this? Basically anything that will allow people to interact and discuss topics other than those strictly linked to work and the project, and which allows individuals to drift from one group to another rather than being assigned to specific people for the duration of the event. If there is an element of fun, the ice will melt even faster. Rather than over-engineering these early-stage events and giving the participants the sentiment that they are being forced to interact, something simple and convivial will probably work best in most environments because this is the setting that will feel natural and will therefore make people feel at ease.

> *The management of people and the creation of an environment that is both embracing and motivating is a responsibility that senior management should take on personally rather than delegating it to external consultants.*

I thought it be worthwhile listing some of the simple, yet effective, activities that I have seen draw project team members together and give them the opportunity to socialise, create a bond, and identify commonality of purpose. I have witnessed this gradual process happening in spite of the diversity of nationalities, functional areas of expertise, and regardless of the company from which they originated. These are only a few examples, but it is easy to see how activities that might have been initially prompted by the senior leadership can rapidly be appropriated by the members of the team and become 'their' thing, part of the cement that defines them as a cohesive team.

■ A deal was set up with a local school to use their sport hall once a week in the evening, so that the project team members who would otherwise merely retire back to their hotel rooms could play basket-ball, volley-ball, badminton or whatever the mood of the week was; play friendly competitions and share some fun. Those who didn't find the energy at the end of the day to play these sports could still come along and cheer their colleagues.

■ A hospitality suite was booked in the hotel in which most of the project team members were staying, to allow them to congregate for a chat or a drink in more private surroundings than the communal areas of the hotel, thereby defining a delineation between the members of the project team and the numerous anonymous other guests in the hotel.

■ Summer picnics were organised in a nearby park. This was incredibly effective because in spite of being simple and inexpensive, there is something festive about an outdoor picnic that spontaneously puts people into a good mood. It is easy for individuals to circulate from one group of colleagues to the next, sit on the lawn or on rugs, and enjoy the total informality of the occasion. Going to the park, enjoying the picnic and returning to the office building probably takes up three hours of one day, so clearly much longer than a normal lunch break. However, the effect on the team and on the number of people who have established new links with their fellow team members is well worth those occasional extra hours. Two or three such event over the course of the sunny season can work wonders on team morale and leave long lasting fond memories.

■ In a similar vein, but requiring less time off and nonetheless giving the team members the opportunity to converse with colleagues with whom they otherwise had little interaction in the project, was to occasionally have a local caterer serve a cooked breakfast buffet in the open plan office space! The cost was moderate, because such caterers are normally busy later in the day serving lunches or dinners, but seldom a breakfast, so this was additional business for them. From the team members' perspective, this big breakfast buffet allowed people stationed in different hotels to all be together and start the day in a fun and unusual way.

■ Possibly the wackiest example of team building and bonding was on a programme I led a few years ago, involving a project team of some 170 individuals from 19 nationalities and very diverse backgrounds, many of them living five days per week on a campus set up in a nearby hotel, and all of them working up to 12 hours a day, and occasionally even longer hours! A Karaoke machine was purchased and connected to a presentation beamer after working hours once a week, providing for many evenings of fun and laughter on Karaoke nights; a perfect opportunity to break down hierarchical barriers and meet project team members from every work stream and every nationality. Cost of the Karaoke machine (including the disks): about $200. Fun value: priceless!

Getting a team to gel rapidly is therefore not a question of big money or great complexity, but rather of creative ideas that avoid that sense of 'déjà vu' and bring an element of fun. It also requires a degree of maturity and confidence from the company's leadership, particularly if the company operates in an environment that has not yet caught onto the fact that highly productive work can be compatible with fun, and where the leadership may fear that the team will spin out of control, lack seriousness, and ultimately fail to achieve its goals.

We all know what 'mature and confident leadership' means, or what it feels like. But to make this meaningful here in the context of merging organisations, in the rest of this chapter I would like to look at some specific criteria that combine to project strong leadership: these are the ingredients of leadership that will allow senior managers to promote this 'comfort factor' of trust and commitment and drive their teams to surpass their limits. I am doing this because few individuals can excel in all of those criteria, but running through this short list can help in identifying areas of particular strength and how to use these knowingly. Conversely it will also serve to build awareness of weaker areas that call for development and will require more effort and focus, and possibly some coaching.

> *Getting a team to gel rapidly is not a question of big money, but rather of creative ideas that avoid that sense of 'déjà vu' and bring an element of fun.*

Building energy, commitment and resilience through strong leadership

Two types of leadership during a business integration

The dual focus of day-to-day business versus integration work calls for two distinct types of leadership.

Once a clear segregation of tasks has been achieved between the teams responsible for on-going daily business and those focused on integrating the two organisations, the individuals in charge of day-to-day business may feel a degree of frustration and stress as a result of things changing gradually around them, but essentially the pressure of work should not be too dissimilar to that of their usual working environment. Those focused on driving the integration process, on the other hand, are constantly faced with issues to resolve, deadlines to meet, and need to be constantly on the alert for new risks or symptoms that might reveal something is not progressing as planned.

Whereas the role of the company's leadership at the most senior level is to continuously remind the organisation of the objective of the integration, paint a compelling picture and make it come to life, the leadership of the teams driving the integration process must get closer to the preoccupations of the team members. Ultimately, these are the people who will either feel compelled to produce extraordinary results, or eventually come to belief they are being driven harshly 'like slave workers' and are being 'used' unfairly by the company.

I have had the privilege of leading teams that performed beyond anyone's expectations, and whose members occasionally openly wondered what had made them accept or even enjoy working so intensely during so many consecutive months. Anyone can take a momentary burst of excess workload, but what keeps some teams going for months on end and still display an amazing level of resilience when others would have long since thrown in the towel? There are, of course, excellent reports and studies of organisational behaviour and team dynamics that explain the mechanisms underlying this collective desire to excel and the mutual commitment team members have towards each other to deliver their common goal[4]. But to keep things straight and simple, I feel that the easiest way to understand what makes people tick and express how they survived the prolonged pressure of their project environment is to pick up a few sound-bites of what they had to say when it was all over.

What we are about to look at here is not a set of capabilities and knowledge of an project leader (such as communication skills, programme management techniques, stakeholder management, analytical skills, intellect etc), which are a pre-requisite for selecting that project leader in the first instance, but rather the way the project leader interacts with the team and manages to motivate each individual in that team through a prolonged period of inordinately intensive work.

General success behaviours versus temperament

The first distinction we need to make when looking at leadership behaviours is between what can be learnt and acquired, emulated, replicated, and what is part of a person's character and personal traits that are not necessarily coachable or trainable for people who don't possess them. I shall start with the general success behaviours that can be replicated, since these can be of help to anyone leading an integration team and there is really no valid excuse for not trying to put these to good use from the early stages of the project through to its conclusion. Here are some of them, together with comments some team members made at the time:

---

[4] To name just a few:

Anne Donnellon : "Team Talk: The Power of Language in Team Dynamics"

Robert J Marshak: "Covert Processes at Work: Managing the Five Hidden Dimensions of Organizational Change"

David K. Carr and Kelvin J. Hard: "Managing the Change Process: A Field Book for Change Agents, Team Leaders, and Reengineering Managers"

■ **Individualised approach**: taking the time to get to know everyone in the team, their strengths, their development areas, their interests. *"This helped everyone know that you cared about them and they could work harder for someone who took an interest in them".*

■ **Social bonding**: ensuring the team can enjoy regular moments of shared social activity to identify commonality and build a bond.*"You ensured that the team had its own Thursday happy hour, you planned spectacular award ceremonies (complete with the perfect award for each person honoured and you in a costume!), the pizza and picnics".*

■ **Role model**: always living up to the highest standards of professional conduct and work ethic; helping team members by working together with them rather than just delegating work to them inconsiderately. *"You were in the trenches (working at a desk in the open area versus in a closed office), demonstrating the kind of work ethic that was necessary for the team to deliver their aggressive goals. This also enabled you to hear the informal conversations and stay in touch with the daily deliverables. Employees saw you working hard and long hours".*

■ **Champion**: being the leader but also the ambassador of the team towards the rest of the company, since it will be necessary to redeploy the team members into the business when the integration project reaches its conclusion. *"You actively championed for your employees to find jobs after [the project] ended. You publicly gave your commitments and followed up on your promises (to the best that [another project] allowed). Your jokes about 'swimming in the talent pool' eased the tension. Employees could relax and deliver the project because they knew that you'd be in their corner when they needed you".*

■ **Clarity and high standards**: *"Everyone knew what needed to be done and when it needed to be completed. You held everyone accountable".*

Looking at the above aspects of leadership behaviours, they all revolve around the notions of reliability, trust, support, consideration, active recognition, and direction, in other words the sentiment that even if the ship needs to fare through a rough storm, the captain at the wheel knows how to manoeuvre it and get everyone to the end destination. And this is of paramount importance in the context of a business integration since typically most people do not know from the onset what that end destination looks like. They expect casualties on the way and fear they might themselves be among those casualties.

Conversely, the integration team cannot be a closed circle of the 'selected few' who are guaranteed a job in the future organisation, come what may. What we are trying to build in the team is a sense of mutual respect, not as a result of hierarchy, but from the acknowledgement of the excellence of everyone's contribution to the project's success. It is a work hard/play hard environment, in which people get a real feeling of 'buzz' from being able to explore new boundaries, learn or develop new skills, get a broader understanding of the business, and contribute through their specialist knowledge and long working hours to the collective success of the team.

At the other end of the spectrum, I have also witnessed projects whose leader's behaviour led the team close to mutiny and rebellion. This came as a result of failing to acknowledge that individuals were working to the very limits of their endurance and considering this to be a perfectly normal pace of work, committing to unrealistic deadlines without any prior consultation with the project team's work stream leaders, adopting a dismissive attitude towards all but a few favourite individuals, and not being their 'champion' when issues were escalated to the Board or when the interests of the project team needed to be represented in the broader organisation.

It might not be in everyone's spontaneous nature to display a supportive coaching style when leading a team, and to those leaders who might feel this would require a constant effort from them, I would strongly advise them that the outcome is well worth the effort. If the person's natural style is perceived to be dry and dismissive (in spite of possibly having the best intentions and a caring nature that fails to express itself convincingly), having a trusted colleague as a sounding board or 'feedback buddy' can make eminent sense, to ensure that the *perceived* behaviour matches what was initially intended.

Temperament

The reason I want to mention temperament as an important factor here is that people may have a few 'natural talents' that are attributes of their personality, most probably shaped by their upbringing, which cannot be learned or emulated by others at short notice, but which provide them with a distinct advantage when it comes to capturing an audience's imagination, stimulating a team, overcoming objection and obtaining people's trust and commitment.

Here are a few such traits of personality that project team members have fed back as attributes that give them cause to respect a leader, enjoy working with that person, and really stretch to the limit of their ability to meet the project's objective and timelines:

- **Charisma and charm**: magnetic personality that people enjoy being around.

- **Sense of humour**: quick witted, with the ability to find the humour in the everyday monotony; not taking oneself too seriously while nonetheless remaining professional in all circumstances at all times.

- **Optimism**: the ability to see the possibilities of a better future and convey them with confidence.

- **Intelligence and worldly perspective**: which inspires confidence and allows team members to expand their professional horizon with an improved understanding of the context in which they operate.

- **Humility**: a nice complement to intelligence so that one does not come across as arrogant; with a measured sense of self-derision, to be able to poke fun at oneself.

- **Being 'real' and approachable**: this requires a mix of candour, openness and patience to create an environment in which team members feel free to express themselves, voice ideas, and occasionally seek support and coaching when things are getting on top of them. This does, however, require that the leader be well organised, or else time might be invested in supporting and coaching team members at the expense of progress on delivering the project.

▌ **Energy and stamina**: energy (not to be confused with 'agitation') is contagious; an up-beat leader sends positive vibes through the project team, and clearly this combination of energy and outstanding stamina is part of leader's responsibility as a role model for the team members – not just "do as I say", but "do as you see me doing". Each of us has a different level of energy, which can fluctuate depending on a number of circumstances. While one cannot *learn* to be energetic, it is certainly possible – and necessary – to get a good grasp of what improves or lowers one's energy level so as to maintain it at an optimal level throughout the integration journey. This may require some adjustments in eating habits (and drinking habits!), physical exercise and other relaxation techniques, posture, organisation of one's daily schedule, hours of sleep per night, or whatever.

The important thing to remember here is that no matter how skilled, well organised, technically competent and amicable the Project Leader is, that person's impact and influence will be seriously impaired if he or she cannot demonstrate sustained high levels of personal energy, and the project team is most likely to underperform in the absence of a strong 'locomotive'.

So what if the Project Leader is not ideal?

Maybe the above headline should not read "what if", because it is almost certain that the person who is available at the right time in the right location to lead the integration will not possess each of the wide range of capabilities, experience, knowledge and personal attributes that are required to be the 'ideal' leader of the integration team.

If the gap is some lack of experience with large complex projects, this can be overcome by having some expert resources in project management, with one very important proviso, which is that this technically less experienced leader will need to focus on energising and driving the team, but will also have to listen and follow the advice given by the project management experts for the daily running of the project!

If the gap relates to some of the general success behaviours listed earlier, it may be necessary for the leader to have one trusted source of feedback, who can hold up a 'mirror' that will allow the leader to make the necessary behavioural adjustments.

Looking at my own experience, under the heading of 'Clarity and high standards' I received the feedback that *"Everyone knew what needed to be done and when it needed to be completed. You held everyone accountable"*. This did not happen without my having to often make a conscious effort to control what would otherwise be my natural behaviour. I sometimes fail to convey my thoughts with clarity because my natural propensity is to 'zap' between several strands of thought, or assume that the people to whom I am speaking are already familiar with the topic. I also tend to speak too fast. All of this concurs to create a tidal wave of information that can potentially cause confusion rather than the clarity I was seeking to provide! Being aware of this and making a conscious effort to bring my natural behaviour under control is highly important, particularly when dealing with new project teams who may shy away from asking questions that might expose their 'ignorance' when in fact those questions would generate very helpful clarification for everyone else in their team. With new teams on new projects, this 'Emperor's New Clothes' syndrome can be avoided by encouraging some candour within the team, making it clear that one is open to receiving feedback that some people might find embarrassing to give.

It is therefore valuable to determine from the onset what weaknesses need to be monitored and be sure to obtain the relevant feedback as soon as possible. Those behaviours of adopting an individualised approach, striving to bond socially, being a role model, providing clarity and living the high professional standards, are very tangible and observable. A good mentor or 'feedback buddy' can easily focus on one or two specific aspects and provide specific feedback on specific behaviours in a given context and the impact of those behaviours on the team members.

> *Determine from the onset what weaknesses need to be monitored and be sure to obtain the relevant feedback as soon as possible*

Receiving continuous feedback and focusing deliberately on improving these weaknesses is most likely to resolve the problem quite rapidly, unless the source of the weakness lies in the person's temperament. In my case, being a hurried person and always wanting to race forwards is what can lead me to 'cutting corners' when giving a briefing. Several years after ending one particularly complex project, I was told by one of the team's senior members: *"In some conversations you tend to assume that your opposite has access to the same amount of information as you do. I was very new when we first met and only knew my [project] world at the time. I remember a number of [occasions] where you walked me through the whole dynamics of the latest Steering Committee meeting assuming I knew everything and everyone. I guess I should have felt comfortable enough to ask questions but for some reason I thought I would figure it out later ".*

The above comment perfectly illustrates the point that I made earlier, which is that in the unfamiliar environment of a new project in which individuals do not know each other well, there will almost always be a reluctance for people to ask questions that might expose their ignorance of a specific topic or their disagreement on a particular subject. Do not, therefore, expect members of the team to spontaneously comment on what they perceive to be weaker areas of their leader, even if this is done in the spirit of supporting a self-development opportunity. My experience has been that one can gain a lot of precious time through self-analysis of one's strengths and weaknesses (based on feedback from previous assignments, or established with the help of a professional coach), and address these openly with the team. In other words: "*I know I tend to do X, which quite often leads to some confusion (or whatever other sub-optimal outcome), so if you catch me doing X please stop me in my tracks and tell me so; this will make working together much easier and more efficient*". This spells out the rules of the game, removes the shyness factor, and demonstrates a degree of openness that is conducive to effective teamwork from the onset.

> *Poor leadership will seriously damage the best organised integration programme but, conversely, strong charismatic and engaging leadership can make up for some imperfections in the way the project is organised or run, because it will fuel the energy, resilience, commitment and willingness within the team to put things back on course.*

Not only on Day One or in the early stages

This might sound like a truism, but there a many things to remember throughout the life-cycle of an integration project, so it's worth repeating here. Remember that the integration journey will feel like a marathon for most members on the integration team: prolonged, and more intense than they thought they could ever endure. As a result, and also because new individuals will join the team as the integration progresses from one stage to the next, the leadership behaviours must be displayed throughout the full duration of the project, not just in the early days. Of the many positive leadership behaviours listed in this chapter, some will come naturally, others will require an effort of self-control. Self-control is difficult to exercise over prolonged periods, and yet this is what will be required from the leader of the integration project team to ensure his or her impact on the team creates the desired outcomes. This is something that is easy to forget during times of stress when the going gets tough and issues accumulate. But remember the skipper in the rowing race: the focus and energy must be continuous or the team will lose its determination to win.

There is always an element of unpredictability when managing an integration. Many components beyond the leadership style will determine how smooth the ride will be, from the quality of the due diligence to the rigour of the planning, staffing of the teams, organisation of the project, involvement of the key stakeholders, communications, and the way the 'soft aspects' are managed. But if you think of these components as a hand of cards, consider leadership style as the ultimate trump card. Poor leadership will seriously damage the best organised integration programme but, conversely, strong charismatic and engaging leadership can make up for some imperfections in the way the project is organised or run, because it will fuel the energy, resilience, commitment and willingness within the team to put things back on course.

In Essence...

▌ *Team cohesion is a prerequisite for the integration team to withstand the prolonged work pressure throughout the project. This cohesion will not happen spontaneously as the individuals in the teams come from diverse backgrounds and would probably not otherwise be working together or have any specific affinity for each other.*

▌ *Creating that sense of cohesion is the responsibility of senior management and should not be delegated to external consultants or contractors.*

▌ *Be aware of the success behaviours and attributes of personal temperament that will help or hinder the way you will lead the integration team or the rest of the company's population through this period of work pressure and uncertainty. Capitalise on your strengths, and identify a 'feedback buddy' or coach to help you adjust your style in your weaker areas.*

▌ *Do not assume that you will easily overcome the weaker aspects of your leadership style: pressure and fatigue will combine to bring out your 'natural style'. You will need a trusted source of feedback to 'hold a mirror up to you', giving you the opportunity to adjust your behaviour and personal impact and thus remain highly effective in driving the team.*

Communication

9

Translating strategy into tangible concepts

Letting them catch up

By the time the decision to buy or merge with another company is reached, the individuals behind this choice have been inundated with facts, data and simulations developed by their advisors and resulting from internal brainstorming sessions they may have run. The helicopter view looks clear; they can envision how the future merged organisation will look and feel. They have thought it through so much, it feels so tangible they can almost 'touch' it.

Not so for the very large majority of people in the company, or in the financial markets, who may have suspected that something was cooking but are now faced with breaking news rather than rumours. What will appear as obvious to the initiators of the merger or acquisition calls for a detailed explanation for all the people who will be affected by this decision. Faced with the daunting task of closing this huge information gap, the temptation is great for the Executive to use as much of the existing material relating to the integration project as is already available. This will, in most cases, be a bad choice! Most of the material prepared during the period leading up to the merger or acquisition decision will have been developed jointly with strategy consultants and other specialised advisors, whose remit was to focus on what would be best for the company, rather than what it will mean for the people working in the company, what is expected from them over the coming year, how it will feel, and what future awaits them after the integration process.

Not only will the whole proposition need to be re-thought and formulated as seen through the eyes of the employees or other stakeholders of the company, but it will take some time and several repeats of the key messages to get the point across.

From the PowerPoint® slide to meaningful words

Busy managers get inundated by a permanent stream of facts and data, and welcome a summary, or better still a one page diagram, that will provide them with a synopsis of what might take five or ten minutes to explain in real words. However, this probably does not apply to the people who are not dealing with abstract concepts and decision processes on a daily basis; and these people may well represent a clear majority of the employee base of a company. I have noticed on numerous occasions that many people struggle to interpret flow diagrams (even in process re-design workshops!), and therefore it is hardly surprising that these same people will not derive much meaningful content from slides that feature lots of text boxes linked to each other by bi-directional arrows.

We have all seen many such slides, but for those not accustomed to this way of presenting concepts and ideas, the result on the audience can only be one of alienation: "I guess they know what they mean, but I don't, so I'll let them get on with it".

Instead of drawing the audience into the forthcoming transformation and making them part of the driving force that will materialise the projected change programme, there is a serious risk of turning them in to passive bystanders, or worse still, sowing the seed of scepticism and resistance as a number of individuals will suspect that the smart over-intellectualised words used in the top management's communication are destined to pull the wool over their eyes and hide something very nasty.

And possibly the most pernicious consequence of using words that are beyond the understanding of a percentage of the audience is that those who do not instantly grasp the meaning of the diagrams and jargon that is presented to them will not ask questions for clarification, from fear of ridicule and appearing unknowledgeable in front of their colleagues and managers, who themselves might not have understood much better.

Coping with the diversity of audiences

Unlike live presentations, which can be very specifically targeted towards clearly defined audiences, written communication is likely to be viewed by a number of readers who do not belong to its primary target audience. With the exception of a few specific presentations and 'road-shows', most of the communication to which the staff of an organisation will be exposed during the course of the integration will be in written form. These can be memos, articles on the company's intranet, house journal articles, posters or slide presentations accessible to general audiences within the organisation. Over-simplifying the terminology used in such documents may be perceived by the readers as reflecting a condescending attitude from senior management. Nobody wants to be considered as ignorant or stupid. Therefore it is worth investing in the work of someone who has extensive experience in such written communication so that the content of all written communication does not end up being over trivialised.

If well managed, written communication offers an opportunity to link the 'consultant jargon' to everyday reality. Those readers who are not accustomed to strategic conceptual language need to find an explanation of strategy statements that will otherwise remain cryptic. A *"What does this mean in practice?"* paragraph will help them grasp what the initial statement means for them, how the content of their job or their future way of working might be impacted.

Those readers who do not need this kind of detailed explanation can skip to the next major statement, and will not mind the fact that superfluous detail is contained in the document provided its structure and presentation are designed in a way that makes it easy for them to skip to the next relevant section without any loss of time.

As the circulation of a piece of written communication broadens across the organisation, individuals who do not belong to its primary target audience will be seeking to decrypt information in messages that were not initially directed towards them. They might even try to speculate and draw conclusions from information that is *not* featured in the written message. This is to the result of the understandable anxiety that is caused by everyone's uncertainty about the forthcoming changes in the organisation. The space for speculation and misinterpretation can be reduced if the communication contains all the facts and considerations that are relevant to a broader audience than the primary target, structured in a way that allows each group of stakeholders to rapidly find the degree of detail and accessibility they require. This is the equivalent of the *"tell me more"* sections we are used to seeing on many websites: individuals who want to know more, or require a more detailed or accessible explanation, must have the possibility of receiving that information.

Defining the future company culture

Diagnosing the starting point

While senior executives can become quite passionate about defining the culture and values of the future integrated company, the 'new world', managing the evolution and transition from what the constituent companies are today towards that envisioned future cannot be achieved unless there is a clear understanding of the journey that needs to be accomplished. And whereas the desired destination is clear, defining the journey that will lead to it assumes, as a pre-requisite, that the starting point is known too. This is the difficult part, because it requires brutal honesty and openness. It requires the candour to recognize that in many (probably most) instances, the culture that prevails in an organisation does not represent a perfect match with its stated values, principles and declared ways of working.

Most companies would like to think that their internal environment is open, honest, encourages communication and trust, supports the development and careers of individuals, and is devoid of internal politics. This is seldom the case, certainly not across an entire organisation – the situation may vary from one business unit to another, or between departments. The greater the desired step change, the more important it will be to have a correct and impartial assessment of the present company culture as it is lived by its employees on a daily basis. By definition, using internal resources to run that assessment will produce biased results, simply because the staff working in areas of the company in which they do not feel they can express themselves openly without adverse consequences will not feel free to report this during the assessment.

This is why even in medium-sized companies it makes sense to ask an external specialised research company to carry out surveys of staff morale and perceptions, all the more so that they have various means of plotting their findings on a graphical scale, which then makes it easier to monitor progress and verify that the steps that are being undertaken to drive the company's culture towards the desired state are effective over time.

Measuring the gap

The diagnosis and mapping of the current culture will reveal the size of the gap that needs to be filled to create the company's targeted culture, as well as the areas in which the efforts will need to be focused. The most commonly used way to express this change, and to make it clear to everyone that this change is a voyage rather than the flicking of a magic switch, is to express it as "from...to": "from individualistic to team-based"; "from hierarchical to collegiate", "from punitive to supportive", "from harsh to fair", "from strong resistance to change, to change is the norm". Conceptually, these 'journeys' sound clear enough for everyone to understand what the company is trying to achieve and how it will feel once that culture becomes embedded into daily life in that organisation. The problem, however, is that in the absence of tangible ways of measuring any progress on that journey, there is a serious risk that the stated desired culture will remain just that: a concept, an intellectualised evocation of what the company's management deems to be the ideal environment. Staff surveys cannot be run at sufficient frequency to allow everyone to appreciate the pace of gradual evolution of the company's culture – nor should they be as this would transform the exercise into a tedious and repetitive task, which will come across as administrative red-tape that merely pays lip service to the wishes of senior management.

So, in the example listed above, how is an individual supposed to assess whether the organisation has indeed become 'more collegial', 'less hierarchical', 'more team-based', 'more accepting of ongoing change'? What would be the manifestations of that evolution? What would be different? The rather subjective perceptions of an organisation being hierarchical, resistant to change, or unsupportive, can be broken down into a subset of clues based on observable behaviours; things one can look out for, which are symptomatic of a specific type of behaviour. This is no different than the statements and questions that appear in the diagnosis questionnaire, except that the questionnaires use cross-examination techniques to measure each behavioural dimension in a number of questions to cancel out the respondents' tendency to bias their answers. Consequently, it should be possible to extract a handful of behaviour indicators from the questionnaire, which can be used to illustrate behaviours that are 'in character' with the target culture, and oppose these to behaviours that belong to the past.

This spells out more clearly the way individuals in the company are required to interact with each other, and what they may expect from each other. Having a tangible way of determining whether a colleague is being exceedingly individualistic compared to the norm the organisation wishes to promote, based on specific observable behaviours and discussing these with that colleagues, is certainly more constructive than simply declaring "you are not a good team player".

Communicating the future culture

Let us be realistic: a culture change takes time and is a journey for everyone. At first, the values and behavioural standards can be little more than words on a page or on colourful posters on display throughout the company. They will only become reality through continual reinforcement.

Communicating the future culture effectively, coherently and in a credible way, requires much more than well-crafted words and visual materials. The real 'proof of concept' can only come from role models, and given that changes in behaviours require a conscious and constant effort until new patterns become truly engrained, most individuals will look 'upwards' in the organisation's structure to check whether their line managers and other layers above them really 'walk the talk' or whether all the ideal behaviours stated in presentations, internal company brochures and colourful posters were just pretty words.

Culture, ways of working and behaviours can be a corner-stone of a step-change in business performance. And where this is the case, senior management need to be made aware from the onset that their ability to conform to the newly-established norms and consistently live the newly stated values will be under constant scrutiny by the rest of the staff. Lapses must be no more than rare exceptions, or else the culture shift will be perceived as being optional and will therefore not take place.

> *Culture, ways of working and behaviours can be a corner-stone of a step-change in business performance. Senior management's ability to conform to the newly established norms and consistently live the newly stated values will be under constant scrutiny by the rest of the organisation.*

Language

Thinking of future translations

Fortunately for Anglo-Saxons, a very large number of business concepts and practices were developed in English speaking countries, so that the terminology used to describe them has been fully integrated into the language. Many of them, such as 'Marketing' or 'Merchandising' have been adopted unchanged by many other languages, simply giving it a gender when required. Marketing thus becomes a masculine concept in French, "Le Marketing", whereas oddly the word that the French tried to promote in the 1970s and 80s to counter the gradual anglicising of their language was the feminine "La Mercatique", which fell into disuse almost immediately.

Life would be very much simpler if each of the business concepts and jargon developed in the past half century in the English language had been taken over by other cultures or had spontaneously found their exact equivalent. But this is not the case. Words abundantly employed such as 'Stakeholder', can only be paraphrased in a number of languages. Likewise with the often quoted notions of 'top-down' and 'bottom-up', 'thinking outside the box', 'ballpark', 'benchmark', '24/7', 'level playing field', 'world class'.

Other English words have, over the years, acquired a distorted meaning in business English. Think of risk 'owners'. Or what about 'we shall take that off-line'.

Translate these expressions into many other languages and the output is most likely to be meaningless. The point I want to make here is that many well crafted crisp and 'to the point' statements written in English are likely to lose their impact when translated into other languages, because in many cases the way one would convey the same message in another language would be based on a very different approach, rather than being a sentence by sentence or even a paragraph by paragraph translation of the original English text. This is relevant particularly in internal newsletters and company in-house magazines, where the layout of the text can be a constraint that causes serious problems as the translated text will in most cases be longer than the English version, precisely because some words need to be paraphrased in the translations. Consequently, some of the text will need to be truncated to fit into the allocated space in the publication and some important information may go missing.

As a non-native English speaker, I am often amused by the translated versions of documents containing business jargon, and particularly company newsletters. One company's annual conference made the headlines of the next edition of its in-house journal, which was due to be published in 12 languages and distributed throughout its divisions and subsidiaries across the world. The French edition was scrapped shortly before it was due to be dispatched, as the heading stating that the company's senior management had drawn key lessons from the past year inferred in the French translation that the senior management had received a spanking they are unlikely to forget!

Releasing poorly translated documents in the sensitive environment of a business integration can be another trigger of 'us and them' feelings that can border on resentment: the recipients of those documents may interpret the sloppy translations as a sign of the senior management's lack of consideration and respect for them, for having not bothered to do a better job in communicating with them.

The best way of preventing such irritating errors from occurring is to provide the translators with a text that is devoid of jargon and buzzwords, or if some of these are unavoidable, to make sure there are some very explicit translation footnotes that will guide the translators in making the right choice of words. The resulting text may appear blunt in English, and quite probably overly verbose, and it would be a shame to deprive the Anglo-Saxon audiences benefit of some of the wonderfully crisp expressions that the English language offers. So what this means in practice is that one often ends up having to write two versions of communication documents: one destined to be used as it is, and the other simplified version destined to be translated without any gross misinterpretations.

Good communications are a time-consuming task. Even though most companies are warned about this, they tend to think that the people who recommend they plan for more resource and time to manage good communications are over-reacting and being fussy. And yet, the ability to formulate well articulated communication during the sensitive months of a business integration is key, as is the capacity to react quickly when unexpected events occur. It is therefore essential to plan for enough time and resource for communications, or to be able to count on the backing of external resources that can be called in at very short notice. Expect *multi-lingual* communication to take you two to three times longer to prepare than a single language campaign, given the need to produce a 'bland' version of each document, have these translated, and cross-check the translators' output.

> *Expect multi-lingual communication to take you two to three times longer to prepare than a single language campaign*

Making life (a little) easier

Because a lot of briefings and other communication exercises in businesses are implemented by way of a cascade that percolates through the layers of the organisation, one way of easing the burden and, more importantly, the dangers of inaccurate translations, is simply to use fewer words, and therefore to use very concise bullet points on presentations rather than complete phrases. This requires the presentations to be accompanied by very comprehensive speaker notes, which will also require translating, but this is an easier exercise than producing translations of final text that are destined to be viewed by the target audience, because any translation inaccuracies or unfamiliar terminology will be detected by the presenters while preparing for the briefing and will be replaced by the expressions that are familiar to their audience.

One slight caveat, however: bullet points do not offer as much context as normal text and are it is therefore more difficult to correctly reflect their meaning in a translation. Consequently, the complete speaker notes need to be written up before the bullet-point slides can be translated, so that the translators can select the correct key words to summarize each point. Again, this needs to be taken into account when planning the time required to produce the presentations because in single-language presentations the speaker notes are very often prepared just before releasing a document. In the case of multi-lingual communications, the translations of the bullet point slides and the adjustment of their lay-out on the slides cannot commence until the speaker notes are available and at least roughly translated.

Delivery

Getting the ducks in a row

It is unlikely at the onset of an integration that everyone in the Executive will fully agree with every point of what the company proposes to do. Nobody can force other people to agree, but for the sake of preserving the coherence of the overall vision and direction, everyone in the Executive will at least have to agree to follow the 'party line' and to adhere closely to the key messages that the communication exercise intends to broadcast across the organisation. Failure to achieve this will result in gaps that will very soon be diagnosed by the sceptics within the audiences, and this will rapidly undermine the credibility of the message for everyone.

When the main axis of the communication have been developed, it is worth running these past the Executives and discussing these in depth to unearth any possible misunderstandings or conflicts of opinion and finding some acceptable resolution before going public. The resolution of diverging opinions may require long discussions or coaching of the 'dissident' Executives, or possibly a re-wording of some of the messages. In either case, skipping over this very important alignment phase through lack of time can have very detrimental consequences. And once again, starting to give some serious through to communications very early in the pre-planning of the integration can pay good dividends.

Difficult where most needed

Presenting in company conventions celebrating last year's excellent results can be great fun and immensely energizing. Standing in front of a crowd of worried employees is less appealing; the natural tendency for most managers will be to procrastinate and only start communicating when it has become absolutely necessary. Business integrations almost invariably end up being good news for a number of employees, and bad news for others. If the cooperation and output of the latter is needed throughout the integration process, there is no other option than to make sure that the communications with that group of individuals are well thought through and delivered to high standards. An unpleasant task, but a necessary one to prevent the target audience's disappointment from turning into resentment, as this would almost certainly have an adverse impact on the company's results or the integration process itself.

As communications cascade downwards through the organisation, it is essential to ensure that the communication plan is adhered to rigorously in the sensitive areas of the company. Involving two or three managers rather than a single individual to deliver together the messages in those difficult pockets of the organisation can help build the confidence and balance that these 'bad news' briefings call for, as well as ensure greater consistency of content and delivery across the business.

It is quite usual for companies to have some divisions or departments in which the staff feel that communication flows well, and others where this is not the case. The audience that feel that communications are poor are precisely those who will require the most attention and support during the integration process. Unless those people feel that way because they were inadvertently left out in previous communication exercises, the reason for their feeling that communications in the company are poor can only be a lack of appropriate skills and confident leadership from their managers. This needs to be acknowledged and resolved when preparing the communication plan for the forthcoming integration: unless these poor communicators are flanked by more experienced colleagues to help them out when the first waves of announcements are made, the situation is likely to worsen.

Skill levels along the communication cascade

Not all created equal

In most companies, senior managers have had numerous opportunities to present to a broad range of audiences and can cope with most situations adequately. Some of them, however, may feel much less confident when presenting messages and painting a picture of a future that might contain elements they themselves find worrying or threatening – will they be able to convey those messages in a factual convincing manner, or will they let their own anxiety transpire in the delivery of the presentation? In case of doubt, it will always be easier for the presenters to work in tandem with at least one other colleague, particularly when it comes to answering questions, because having two or three to deliver a complex and potentially delicate message provides the speakers with enough time to formulate their answers during 'questions time'. It also allows the other colleagues to re-position some statements in case anything that was said could be misinterpreted – the presenters can build on each other's statements and comments and together give a stronger sense that this is the 'voice of the company' rather than one single individual's interpretation of the situation.

It is worth pointing out here that the 'Questions & Answers' sheets that usually flank a communication pack should, in addition to providing a ready-made standard and coherent answer to questions that are likely to be raised in the audience, also serve to ensure unequivocal understanding of the core messages and implications by the people who will be presenting the briefings, so as to prevent any personal bias when the messages are being delivered.

A cascade of face-to-face team briefings are a powerful means of percolating key messages through the layers of an organisation because they provide something no carefully written and translated message from headquarters can achieve: local commitment and a connection of the message to the people through people. They have the ability to hit the right button in terms of 'what does this mean for us' and 'what's in it for me'.

The exercise may become increasingly difficult as the presentations cascade through the layers of the organisation: the briefings reach the less senior levels of the company, those presenting will be less experienced while the exposure of their audiences to the forthcoming changes grows. The questions asked by the audience will relate less to the strategy, concepts and principles that formed the core of the presentation's content, and more to concrete situations that will present themselves in daily life during and after the integration. It is not fair to expect a junior manager or shop-floor team-leader to manage such a briefing without being flanked by a few colleagues. Some of them will, of course, fare really well through this experience, but many of them will most probably not, and this is what really matters. The recipients of incomplete or inconsistent or non-convincing communications will coalesce as many pockets of inertia during the integration process – people who will not have any clarity as to what will happen, when it will happen, why it will happen, what will be expected from them, and why it is worth them making that effort. Coming back to my analogy of the eggs and oil in a bowl, this is when you may see the first signs of your mayonnaise beginning to curdle …

Asking middle and junior managers and team leaders to lead such communication briefings puts them on the spot, but with the support of one or two peers they will not feel they have been dropped into a lion's cage, and the confidence of that support is likely to help them perform very well. This transforms a difficult exercise into a valuable learning experience. Not only does the pairing of presenters prevent the shortcomings that might result from any individual's inexperience or lack of skill, but it actually provides a perfect real-life training ground for these presenters to develop and gain confidence. I have seen numerous junior managers and team leaders come out of what they expected to be difficult briefings with a feeling of tremendous relief: "it went much better than I'd expected" is the usual comment, and beyond that feeling of relief is a sense of achievement. Importantly too, the direct involvement of middle-managers in the communication process and the satisfaction they can get by performing well in this new and difficult role prevents them from being mere bystanders during the company's integration journey. They might not be directly in the 'driver's seat' as most of the key decisions are made at a higher level of the organisation, but they are nonetheless important co-pilots and as such share the responsibility for the final outcome.

Using several media

As a communication exercise cascades down the organisation, geographical distance and the number of simultaneous briefings make it virtually impossible to ensure with certainty that each briefing will have adhered strictly to the pre-agreed content, style and format. For the sake of coherence and reinforcement of the messages, it is therefore worth considering the use of a number of media that will complete each other and, when necessary, adjust what an inexperienced or immature manager may have conveyed during an oral briefing. In this way, each individual will have been exposed to the key messages from a variety of sources. Among the many possibilities for such communications reinforcement, let us mention the company in-house journal, intranet website, desk drops, posters, CDs, DVDs, or live events such as 'Questions & Answers' breakfasts, lunch breaks or teleconferences.

The objective would be to make it almost impossible for anyone not to have been exposed to at least two or three sources of information that convey a coherent message.

Remember to give some thought to who the indirect target audience might be, because these are individuals who may also relay and reinforce your core messages. During a recent merger I led, a DVD with multi-lingual sound tracks was given to some 2,000 employees across Europe shortly before Day One, containing a motivational presentation of the company and its new vision, interviews of the members of the Executive, and short statements by numerous employees based in a variety of locations. The DVD was designed to provide a good overview of the diversity, increased scale and competitive strength the company had reached with the merger. Whereas printed house journals tend to be read in isolation during a lunch break, the recipients of the DVD gathered with family and friends in front of their television set in the evening to view it. This allowed discussion and debate to take place within each person's family circle. It promoted better understanding by all family members of what the employees had lived through over the past few months, and projected a reassuring picture of the future. The DVD generated very positive feedback and went a long way towards appeasing some of the anxiety that had built up within the company over the previous few months.

The message versus the words that were spoken ...

It might sound incredibly obvious to say that the words used to communicate a particular idea or vision to an audience of senior managers are not the same that will resonate with people who are closer to the shop-floor. Getting the message across is essential, but use of business jargon will alienate shop-floor audiences, whereas paraphrasing concepts that could be encapsulated in one word will feel very condescending to a more senior crowd. And yet, many companies miss the opportunity to choose the correctly crafted words for their various audiences, and the reason for this is that they will not have allowed enough time to adjust the language to their diverse audiences.

Choosing the right words using the language and expressions that are well established in the operating environment in which the message is being delivered is also crucial to convey authenticity. Without that sense of authenticity, the message cannot reach the hearts and minds of the target audience. This has important implications on the depth of the briefing that must be given to the people in charge of communications during the integration project. This might be an external agency, making the need to adjust the vocabulary, mood and tone of the messages even greater.

This adaptation exercise might not feel too difficult in the early phases of a project, particularly just before the real integration effort enters its main implementation phases. But once the integration process has actually begun, a large number of people throughout the company will be subject to an overall workload that brings them close to breaking point. Unless the communications team is sufficiently resourced, this will not be the right time to ask anyone to urgently proof-read communication briefs, correct them where appropriate and provide any relevant comments.

This comes back to the question of time planning: communications will almost always require far more time and resource than one's most pessimistic forecast, and the rule of thumb for multi-lingual communications is that the timeline will increase threefold, or at the very least be doubled.

Being visible

Credibility

In spite of carefully crafted communications and well delivered presentations, the key hurdle that needs to be overcome, from the moment two companies declare their intention to integrate until the first tangible signs can be felt that they are beginning to operate as one, is that of scepticism: *"Nice words – but is this not Management playing lip-service to the people at the top of the pyramid?"*.

Quickly delivering the message and then disappearing behind the trenches will be perceived by the receiving audiences as management hiding away from the truth, or not being able to face everyone in the eye. And therefore, conversely, the only way to demonstrate honesty and openness is to remain visible in the days that follow the communication briefings: visible to answer questions, to develop in a more specific way some of the topics discussed in the initial briefings, but also visible to display positive behaviours, confidence, energy and belief in the plan that was exposed during the briefing.

Walking the floor is also quite possibly the best way of gleaning feedback and taking the pulse of the organisation – be it verbally through questions people might ask when they get to see their manager walking through their department, or through the general atmosphere reigning in the office or shop-floor. But even for those individuals who might not feel comfortable going up to a manager they see walking across their department or shop floor, the mere fact that this person is there rather than hiding away in an office demonstrates that management is not shying away from its responsibilities and is keen to remain 'in touch'.

What about some fun...

I know this may sound like a tall order for some people, but in my experience an effective way of positioning an integration as a positive exercise, rather than merely attempting to calm down people's anxiety, is to emphasize the uniqueness of the experience and presenting it as something that can actually be fun. Think of a wedding. In today's world, half of all marriages sadly end up in divorce, but in spite of the high level of risk that such a venture represents, a wedding is always a cause for big celebration, joy and optimism; an opportunity to envisage the future, its challenges and rewards. The event is unique, it marks a new beginning, the start of a new life. The successful marriage requires efforts on both sides, but conventional wisdom tells us that the rewards are well worth those efforts. Why should we treat the coming together of two companies any differently? Particularly if we have decided from the onset to execute the integration in the right way and therefore be part of the 20% of mergers and acquisitions that will fulfil their promise to deliver value?

A business integration can be fun because it breaks away from routine, it is an unexpected learning experience. It is stimulating because it keeps people on their toes. It brings people together because they will need to work hard together, think fast and react swiftly to unexpected events. And just as in the teams that work hard together in college or university to prepare for challenging exams, the teamwork that takes place during a business integration usually builds a strong bond between the members of the project teams, and also brings people together across the entire business. This is because at some point they will have to help each other out, adapting their ways of working, developing new skills, learning new techniques, adopting new house-rules, interfacing with new colleagues.

Personally, I have always adopted this approach with the integration project teams, from the very first briefing they receive. I think the message they retain from that first briefing must be something like "I know you may find it hard to believe now, but very soon you will realise that integrating two organisations can be fun and very exciting". And with the exception of a few individuals (who are probably very difficult to amuse and excite!), this has worked very well because it very clearly re-positions a potential threat into something that will be a fantastic opportunity for most of them, something positive to look forward to.

Living the fun

The whole notion of giving some levity to the integration process and positioning it as a positive opportunity assumes that activities and small events are planned along the way to celebrate achievements and share some fun. Many companies forget to do this, arguing that they do not have an entertainment budget that could support such activities. Having fun and celebrating success does not mean holding a huge office party. It is more about acknowledging the little steps of regular progress, the achievement of milestones along the long path of integration. Acknowledging individuals for a particular contribution. It is not about big money and bonuses, but more about acknowledgement and personal consideration.

Business literature does not pay much attention to the subject of *laughter*, and in most instances that laughter is linked to a notion of ridicule and mockery, such as in *"laughable results"*, rather than to the sense of release, celebration and enjoyment that is well deserved after a job well done. Laughter and fun are a powerful relief for the stress and fatigue that inevitably affect the members of a project team as a result of very long working hours and repeated overnight stays in hotels. Acknowledging that special effort by allowing people to share some fun and let their hair down gives life on a project a welcome human touch. It also allows team members to get to know each other in a more informal setting, which can lead to more effective teamwork when the fun is over and everyone gets back to work. The karaoke machine that was used during a particularly strenuous programme I led in the United States was a fine example of how some 170 individuals from different horizons, nationalities and social backgrounds could remain together after their very long working hours to share some fun. When all the hard work and sweat is over, it is the fun moments people will remember.

Fun can also be combined with recognition, and makes for longer lasting memories in people's minds. Rather than reading out a list of individuals the company has singled out for outstanding achievements, one large project I ran in North America organised an Academy Awards' Oscar night, fully fledged with members of the project's management team wearing tuxedos or full length sequined evening dress to host the event in true Hollywood style. Beyond the amusing and unusual theme of the event, an Oscar ceremony allowed many people to be acknowledged in that large project team, given that for each Oscar category a number of people could be 'nominated'; each of the nominees being tied to a film whose title, story-line or style befitted that person's role or achievement on the project. That Oscar night caused roars of laughter and mutual cheering. The fake Oscar statuettes purchased in a souvenir shop had cost very little compared to more conventional company gifts, for which we had no budget to spend anyway. But they proudly adorned the desks of the winners for several months, whereas more traditional and serious-looking 'Company Award" certificates might have landed directly in a drawer.

When it comes to fun, ideas and originality can often produce better results than big money.

If the boss is worried, I should be too

In any communication campaign, the information that appears to have the highest value to individuals is whatever was *not* included in the official messages. The scoop, what management may have refrained from divulging. In the sensitive environment of a company integration, people will tend to be on the lookout for any indices that may hint that the reality might not be as rosy as depicted in the management's statements. Body language will be keenly observed to detect clues of a mismatch between the official party line and what is actually going on backstage.

While in a well orchestrated integration individuals would be assigned to focus on either the integration project or the running of daily business, the members of the Executive have no other choice than to be involved in both. The inevitable consequence of this dual responsibility is very long days and rather short nights, the physical impact of which is likely to become visible after a few months. Looking a little drawn and tired is quite understandable, but the other more significant consequence of fatigue is that one tends to become a little withdrawn, less communicative, move introvert as one's mind struggles to process the inordinately heavy workload. This is when people in the company will begin to worry, as they see a senior manager walk across the office hardly making eye contact with anyone, not sharing a few words with some of their colleagues, or forgetting to even say hello. Something must be wrong, the boss is worried and so should I be.

The remedy can be simple: smile! Very easy to do, and sounds rather trivial, but unfortunately very easy to forget when one is feeling the effects of lasting work pressure. Smile, say hello, shake hands with people in cultures where this would be expected, and exchange a few words, even if that means that crossing the office floor will take two minutes longer – they are well invested. Assuming that the management's communication campaign is honest, the only way for the staff to acknowledge this honesty is to perceive the senior management team as being approachable and open, and if the boss looks a little tired but is still smiling, one can only conclude that things must be under control. I actually find smiling has a positive impact on my own mental disposition, as well as being reassuring and energising for those around me. Smiling is communicative and contagious – smile at someone and they will usually smile back. When life gets as pressured as it can be during business integration, the daily sight of smiling faces is very welcome!

The other non-verbal signals

If smiling during tough times is relatively easy, maintaining one's composure under stress is a bigger challenge. Again, fatigue, pressure, mental overload act together and bring individuals close to their limits – or maybe beyond. Patience becomes very limited, small irritating events can blow out of proportion. If the situation gets such that a member of the Executive needs to 'let off steam', it had better be behind closed doors or else the positive picture conveyed in the carefully crafted company communication will have lost all credibility. Self-control is therefore absolutely key.

There is no universal antidote to prevent lasting stress from impacting one's temper. For many people, a solid programme of physical exercise throughout the integration programme will help them keep their mental balance – having a good sweat at the gym is one good way of getting things out of one's system. Some individuals may opt for a healthier diet that could help their body stand the strain of their workload. Others might include a high priority time-slot in their daytime or evening schedule for some pleasurable and relaxing activity; this could be playing a musical instrument, performing a yoga routine or any suchlike interest that provides a complete break from the work rhythm and preoccupations of the project. Whatever is appropriate for a particular individual to alleviate part of the wear and tear caused by prolonged work pressure, one needs to give it some serious consideration and plan for it ahead of time, because once activity levels reach a peak during the integration process there will be no time nor mental bandwidth to think about what relaxing and healthy activities will provide the release required to maintain mental balance.

Having a good coach can also be an excellent way of reducing anxiety and stress, it provides a sounding board by having someone external to the organisation with whom one can exchange ideas without being assessed; someone on whom one can 'off-load' when the going gets tough. That coach will be able to hold up a mirror by giving constructive feedback and advice to those senior executives who have trouble projecting a body language that comes across as energetic and confident. This energy and confidence are the signals people will be seeking when they observe their top managers, as a confirmation of the positive messages conveyed in the company's communication. Getting this right is therefore key.

Does this resonate?

Not one size fits all

Because people may feel alienated at the onset of a business integration, with a sense of loss of control over their professional life, unless something within the communication they receive really strikes a chord and is perceived as being particularly relevant, standardised messages will only reinforce that feeling of being one helpless anonymous soul within a large crowd of strangers. Relevance ensues from content, but also from style. Placing the message within the specific context of a set of stakeholders is the necessary condition for it to be credible and tangible. Choosing the right vocabulary and terminology will reinforce the audiences' sense that the messages are destined specifically for them. All of this is plainly obvious, but I allow myself to mention it as a reminder, and more particularly to demonstrate why an effective communication campaign will invariably require more resources than one would initially expect. One same set of core messages will need to be adapted over and over again, sometimes just a slight tweak, to ensure that the audiences instantly recognize that their specific circumstances are being addressed, and therefore remain focused on the content of those messages that they will retain through associations with situations of their everyday life.

> *Relevance ensues from content, but also from style. Placing the message within the specific context of a set of stakeholders is the necessary condition for it to be credible and tangible*

Does my idea look big in this?

One of the aspects through which an audience will sense whether a message was crafted specifically for it or just rolled-out in a standardised way is the balance between conceptual and pragmatic argumentations, particularly in the answer to the very basic question of "why are we doing this?". In fact, from an individual's perspective, there are three questions that need to be answered repeatedly to ensure the messages really sink in:

- Why are we doing this?

- What is expected from me?

- How will it feel?

Failing to answer the first of these questions makes the other two quite irrelevant. Justifying the reasons for a major acquisition or merger, and the reasons for the need to change, can be done in a number of ways, which range in a continuum from the highly conceptual approach based on economic data and market trends to the more down-to-earth narrative that draws on analogies with everyday life and plain common sense. Finding the appropriate point along that continuum is key for the individuals in each audience to have clarity about why the companies need to integrate, why this is the best course of action over other options, why it is important for them to be fully on board, what contribution is expected from them to achieve a successful integration, and what the journey will look like.

In Essence...

■ *Formulate your proposition as seen through the eyes of the employees or other stakeholders of the company, using their terminology and tangible examples to which they can relate.*

■ *Seek relevance - "what's in it for me?" and generate involvement:*
"why are we doing this?" "what is expected from me?", "how will it feel?".

■ *Remember your communication may reach a broader audience than your primary target.*

■ *Communicate culture and values through observable behaviours, which need to be lived by senior management as role-models.*

■ *Think of foreign language translations: prepare comprehensive explanatory notes to ensure translation accuracy; the timeline to prepare multilingual versions will extend two or threefold compared to single language communication.*

■ *Pair up less experienced presenters to deliver the communication in tandem; involve middle management and team leads in percolating the communication through the layers of the company.*

■ *Use several channels of communication to allow multiple exposure to your messages.*

■ *Be aware of your body language: is it as positive as the messages in your verbal communication?*

The Future Team

How revolutionary?

Seizing the opportunity

One of the most exciting opportunities offered by company mergers or significant acquisitions is the chance to redefine the fundamentals of the business, make a quantum leap rather than incremental change, shift the paradigm. It would be incredibly difficult to find a detonator for such radical transformation in an on-going business, unless this were imperatively required to prevent an imminent collapse of a company. By contrast, the integration of two companies opens doors to a new world, to something that is not necessarily a balanced combination of Company A and Company B, but which departs from previously known patterns to explore new ways of working.

The idea sounds a little scary, because it comprises more risk than an evolutionary approach, but conversely the prize can be bigger, particularly if one or both of the constituent companies presented a few 'anomalies', a negative heritage from the past that is difficult to shake away and may call for more abrupt change to part with the past and face a fresh new future.

Given the uniqueness of the opportunity, it would be a great shame not to at least consider the pros and cons of radical change in some degree of detail in the very early stages of the planning phase, or indeed before the merger or acquisition decision is finalised. Significant change to the company's business model and/or organisation structure may have a very significant impact on the merger's business case, and sometimes boldness pays dividends.

Why *must* it be so new?

American wisdom tells us that *"if it ain't broken don't fix it"*. In my experience, most companies find it difficult, when planning their integration, to resist the urge to change at least 'something'. I have seen companies based on a functional structure suddenly opt for a matrix organisation, as well as a multi-national whose organisation was based on geographical regions re-classify its markets by degree of maturity and opportunity rather than by continental area, only to re-discover the practicality of a geographically based structure a few years later and switch back to a structure that was strangely similar to what it was prior to the merger...

A number of factors can lead to this urge to change. Firstly, senior management is by definition action-oriented and it's role is to create value: changing an organisation makes their impact visible to the world at large, whereas leaving things as they are could be interpreted as a 'wait and see' or indecisive attitude.

A second plausible explanation - possibly a little more cynical but not totally unreasonable - is that more change requires more support to be implemented, and therefore bringing on change for the sake of change can also allow the consultants and numerous contractors that normally accompany a business integration to profile themselves and generate lucrative assignments: a change manager's dream!

Whatever the true motives behind such change, there is one undeniable positive fact about them, which is that they mark the beginning of a new era. They are a way of creating a virtual partition line between the past and the future. The way we were, and the way we want to be from now on. They mark a determination to shape a different future and reinforce the notion that merely doing more of what we used to do will not deliver the ambitious goals the company has set for itself.

Bold and bolder

If *some* degree of change can prove necessary in putting a virtual stake in the ground and marketing the beginning of a new era, companies would be wise to remember that any more profound change in their organisation structure will require the support of very experienced resources and will possibly consume a high proportion of management's time and effort to implement.

The real risk comes from the fact that many operational changes will be taking place at the same time. These can be systems changes, a transformation of the supply chain, a re-modelling of the manufacturing footprint, the introduction of new processes and controls, relocation of offices etc. These require a serious effort from all individuals concerned to adapt to the new work environment; changing the reporting lines and organisation structure while people are struggling to familiarise themselves with new ways of working may lead to operational failures that will be all the more difficult to prevent or manage because numerous individuals with still be unclear about their remit and responsibilities and will be unfamiliar with the people with whom they need to interface to resolve these operational problems.

Quantum leap versus staggered approach

The simplest way of avoiding 'change overload' and preventing events from spinning out of control is to implement the overall changes in two or three stages. I emphasize the word 'stages' by opposition to a continuous evolution, because this notion of 'before the change' and 'after the change' is important. Continuous evolution would cause confusion and give the impression that everything is in constant flux. Stages, by opposition, assume that everyone is aligned at the end of one stage before passing onto the next.

One important caveat, however. In terms of communications, stages of change must be positioned exactly as such: a temporary step towards a destination that must be known from the onset. Failure to get this clarity in everyone's mind would result in a perception that one change did not produce the desired effect and is therefore being changed again, and again, and again... Stages, in contrast, set a clear overall direction but recognize that people have a certain bandwidth of acceptable on-going change, and that progressing in pre-defined steps will help make the overall journey more bearable.

The corollary of this is that when one stage is almost completed, it is necessary to re-emphasize repeatedly what the final desired outcome is, so that people remain aligned and focused on the aim of the company's transformation and do not begin to settle in the pattern resulting from one of the intermediate stages.

The fewer the stages can be, the better. Proceeding by relatively small increments will only extend the overall duration of the journey and almost inevitably cause change fatigue. Let us bear in mind, as explained right at the beginning of this book, that speed matters. Speed, tempered by feasibility.

The right person in the right role

What type of hole for the square peg?

Organisations continuously attempt to morph, so as to adapt to their environment and anticipate the future, as well as to make the best use of the resources upon which they can draw. This is the result of trying to do the best with what one has, an expression of pragmatism and an attempt to avoid wastage. Over time, the remit of many individuals reflects their particular attributes and skills, and unless a company sticks to very rigorous job descriptions and organisation structures, over time one can observe that the structure ends up fitting the individuals, rather than the other way around, as a result of which various subsidiaries of one same company will present a variety of incomparable organisation structures.

As managers join and leave a company, the quest for a successor to fill a vacancy often finds an easy solution when the remit of an internal candidate can be expanded to close the gap. Over time, unless a formal reorganisation is undertaken, reporting lines and the actual remit of many senior positions in a company can look surprisingly illogical, and only make sense because of the experience and skill-sets of the individuals who occupy those roles and for whom the structure will feel appropriate.

This makes me think of those comfortable shoes that gradually take the shape of the feet inside them and can end up looking quite unlike what they were initially in that shop window, but they are still so comfortable! Under normal circumstances, there is no sense in my view in being dogmatic about organisation structures: the key aim of an organisation is to be effective and in some cases this requires adapting the model to a reality that does not match the perfect textbook model. And so the Hungarian sales subsidiary of a Europe-wide company might report into the European Supply Chain Director just because the latter happens to be able to speak Hungarian, Polish and Ukrainian.

However, the situation changes significantly when two organisations need to be merged. Instinctively, there is a tendency to think of specific individuals and then try to imagine how best to fit them in a future organisation. "We have two capable Supply Chain Directors, but maybe if we divided the European region into two or three areas, the European Supply Chain Director who speaks Hungarian, Polish and Ukrainian could make an excellent Regional Director for Central and Eastern Europe...".

The vast majority of studies and books on organisation are adamant about the fact that it is the individuals that need to fit into jobs, rather than jobs being crafted around individuals. I fully agree with that approach and shall not run through the complete argumentation, which has already filled many books. But the key question is: how does this work in reality?

If only a handful of key individuals are likely to be assigned to posts that do not fully match their comfort zone, it may be worth going ahead with the plan and providing those specific individuals with additional support and coaching to help them grow into their newly defined role.

This will clearly not work if a significant number of managers with key knowledge are being considered for roles in which they will feel very uncomfortable. Just as squeezing square pegs into round holes will end up in breakage, enforcing an organisation structure that is a mismatch for a significant number of key players will cause pain and result in a dysfunctional organisation. So do we opt for another organisation design, or accept the need to change the people after all?

Don't leave me now

In some cases, there may be good reasons to justify a radical change and bring some 'new blood' into the organisation. If the talent that is sought for is available on the market and the cost of the change is affordable, this can be a plausible scenario. However, the leavers may include a number of people the company would have much preferred to retain. Organising a well-structured knowledge transfer is time consuming and potentially very costly, but the prize may be worth it. That cost will include recruitment fees, the cost of having two incumbents in one same role during the knowledge transfer period, which can extend over one to six months, as well as a retention bonus for the leaver, the magnitude of which will depend on the length of the transition period, which itself is a function of the duration of the knowledge transfer period, but also of the recruitment process that precedes it. Depending on the market conditions and the levels of skill and experience required in the recruitment brief, this can end up being a surprisingly long period.

Orderly integrations require speed: getting rapidly to a stage where everyone has clarity on his/her role and how it interfaces with others in the company is key – that clarity is the prerequisite for efficiency and focus. This does not mean that one has accepted to compromise on the opportunity to establish the optimal structure for a company: the initial post-integration structure can be a temporary step that provides an interval of time during which plans can be fine-tuned to evolve into the second stage of organisational change.

In, out, or not sure?

The Day One trinity

Naming the CEO is the obvious first step of any merger integration; quite often the decision on who will lead the integrated company is a core part of the acquisition or merger negotiation. Some companies opt for a CEO and Deputy CEO duet to head the company, which can help in projecting some sense of 'balance' to those who fear that their company's identity and values will be lost in the integration process. In addition to this, having two individuals at the top of the organisation can allow the CEO to focus on shaping the company to deliver its future strategy, while the Deputy CEO concentrates on maintaining the daily business on track during the start of the integration and delivering the companies' current budgets: even during the toughest of integrations, there is no mercy for companies who fail to hit their numbers...

But in all honesty, Deputy CEOs are not expected to serve much longer on the Company's Executive team than is absolutely necessary to ensure a smooth commencement of the integration process. And even in cases where the CEO and Deputy CEO had expected to co-exist for quite some time, as the integration progresses decisions need to be made regarding a number of principles on which the two individuals at the top of the hierarchy are unlikely to agree. At that point, one of them – usually the Deputy CEO – will have step down to avoid ambiguity that would be detrimental to the business's stability and development. Which is why so often carefully crafted press announcements are made about "diverging views on future strategy" when one of the men at the top leaves the company to pursue other interests.

Most CEOs are obsessed with quickly sorting out who will be in what role in the upper echelons of the organisation, which is understandable as vacancies at the top will, over time, undermine accountability, paralyse action and can place the organisation in a state of flux. In an ideal world, if all the members of the integrated company's Executive can be nominated and announced prior to Day One, all the better. In publicly quoted companies, this would be the norm, even if the Executive team is expressly announced as a transition team: the investor community will want to know who is in control, who is accountable, and for this they need to see names and faces.

Companies that are not quoted on a stock exchange can afford more flexibility if they have closer ties and a relationship of trust with their shareholders, as the latter will understand that sorting out the Executive team appointments in great urgency and having to revise it subsequently can in itself cause negative shockwaves across the company. Nonetheless, the *principles* underlying the way the new team will be selected, and the layers beneath it, must be clear from the onset, and one individual needs to be the custodian of those principles and carry the full accountability of ensuring compliance with them. Beyond the appointment of the CEO, it is therefore crucially important that the head of Human Resources function be appointed in time to be fully operational on Day One. It is preferable for this to happen much ahead of Day One given the amount of preparation required in the human resources arena before the integration can commence, but in the worst case Day One must be considered as the absolute deadline for the appointment of this individual.

The other role that needs to be in place by Day One at the latest is that of the Finance Director, because of the complexity of the work that needs to be carried out in the Financial area to integrate two companies, but also and primarily because of the accountability the Company's CFO needs to bear to satisfy the requirements of Compliance and Governance.

The CEO, CFO and HR Director represent the minimum core of the initial Executive team. The other roles can either be temporarily nominated, particularly in publicly quoted companies, or left vacant at first in private companies. It is more important on Day One to have clearly defined principles of how the staffing of key positions will be decided, than to have names in every single box of the organisation chart, particularly as some names may change along the way if someone nominated to a key position does not accept the offer! The staff in the organisation will find it more logical that some key positions are yet to be filled, rather than see names change in the first weeks of the organisation, revealing some degree of dysfunction and faction struggles among their leaders.

Having the CEO, CFO and HR Director in place on Day One provides clear accountability for what will happen during the following steps of the integration, while still affording the time to make the right decisions along the way, rather than hasty nominations that are designed merely to project a sense of clarity but might well end up being the wrong ones for the company's best interests.

Safeguarding the 'sacred cows'

Most companies do not like to admit this, as the very concept of having 'sacred cows' in an organisation flies in the face of best practice in Organisation Design. Reality can tend towards best practice, but seldom matches all the criteria, and therefore when two companies merge, particularly private companies, there are a few individuals to whom the respective companies (or their owner) feel they owe a favour. This may be because of their special contribution in making the company what it is today, or just out of loyalty because they have been around for many years and become part of the very fabric of the company over time.

In many cases, as a result of their many years of service, these individuals are likely to be earning a significantly higher remuneration package than other staff with similar qualifications, which can of course be a problem when one is trying to blend two organisations into one while optimising the structure's costs and effectiveness. On some occasions, circumstances over the years can lead some of these individuals to being over-promoted, or being given special functional titles which acknowledge that their previous company viewed them as 'special' but that are hard to match in a new integrated structure.

Whatever the reasons for these people's special status, their uniqueness poses a threat to an orderly staffing process or even to a coherent organisation design. In the absence of a few agreed principles regarding the treatment of the companies' sacred cows, there is a risk that senior management will feel compelled to offer far more generous severance terms to those individuals than the scheme agreed for the rest of the new company. This creates inequalities and a dangerous precedent. The alternative is to shoehorn some of the sacred cows into a few 'special roles' created in the new organisation. Best practice says this should never happen. Reality, on the other hand, shows us that at least a few of these sacred cows have a degree of business knowledge that will be very valuable in the integrated organisation, at least in its early stages until a proper knowledge transfer process can have taken place.

Recognising the transient value of this knowledge in an open way will help senior management safeguard the sacred cows that are worthy of such differentiated treatment during the resourcing process. It will also justify any 'golden parachute' that is granted to them subsequently. They will have played a decisive and valuable role in the successful integration of the two companies, either by transmitting their knowledge to their successor, or by accepting a less privileged role and its associated remuneration package within the ordinary resourcing process, just like anyone else in the company. The latter usually only works well for individuals who are nearing retirement and wish to remain active professionally without seeking new career opportunities in other companies. For others, who still aspire to a number of years of professional challenge and recognition, taking advantage of the golden parachute and seeking happiness elsewhere is likely to be the preferred outcome.

To ensure the situation remains manageable, it is therefore well worth defining from the onset who are the sacred cows, what makes them sacred, and agreeing on a maximum quota of such individuals that each of the companies can invoke within the staffing process. In larger companies, some of the sacred cows need to be safeguarded for 'political' reasons, but in the mass of the organisation these can go relatively unnoticed and there can always be some temporary explanation to justify their presence in the early months of the new integrated company. This issue can become far more acute in small and medium sized companies, because in organisations of that size, many members of management and staff can have close personal ties with the boss or owner of the company, which go well beyond an employer/employee relationship, and involve a degree of friendship or at least mutual loyalty.

An attempt to merge two small companies (each with under 50 staff) both of which had a long history as family-owned businesses and had just been acquired by large international groups, was aborted precisely because of the excessive number of sacred cows that one of the companies had invoked. These represented too high a percentage in relation to the total number of staff and could clearly not all be considered as exceptions; this jeopardized the organisation design of the integrated company and the whole merger project was finally aborted. The above events took place in the early 1990s, and it is likely that in our current days of tougher business the two parent companies would have intervened to impose more rational thinking in assessing the suitability of the two companies for the future integrated organisation. But in those days it was deemed that the degree of personal loyalty and camaraderie that bound the staff and senior management was such that upsetting that unusual balance would have destroyed the fabric of the organisation and, potentially, its ability to succeed on the market.

Dealing in an honest and fair way with the sacred cows is what many senior managers will find the most difficult part of an integration because the choices are tough: nobody likes to have to choose between a friendship and the imperatives of the business, reconciling the two requires good preparation. Imagine the various courses the conversation with each of these individuals might take. Will this come as a total surprise or will they have somehow sensed that their special status may be in jeopardy? Will they have some understanding for the circumstances that have led to the situation the business is now facing, or will they feel betrayed and rejected? How open might they be to transition roles and will they see these in a positive light?

Astonishingly, I have witnessed several cases in which the commiseration was in reverse compared to what might be expected, and where the recipient of the bad news ends up reassuring the friend who had to break the news that everything will be alright and that they fully understand and accept the logic that led to the decision. A deep sigh of relief when things happen this way, although this is indeed the exception rather than the rule!

In Essence...

■ *How radically different will the new integrated organisation be compared to the former two companies? Do you want to implement a quantum leap, or roll-out the change in several stages?*

■ *Make sure the CEO, Finance Director and Human Resources Director are nominated in advance of Day One. The other members of the Executive can conceivably be transition roles until the final incumbents are nominated.*

■ *Fit individuals into roles, rather than create roles for individuals.*

■ *Some individuals (sacred cows) may need to be retained during a transition period even though they do not fit a role in the new structure: these should remain exceptions and be justified by some specific capability or knowledge.*

■ *The transient nature of the sacred cows must not be allowed to become permanent: this assumes knowledge transfer plans are in place to allow the new organisation to take over after the initial transition period.*

Wrapping-up the Integration Project

Why so important?

Getting closure

> *The sooner the customers and the company's products or services can return to the centre of the radar screen, the better.*

Communications during the integration process will have shown everyone the light at the end of the long tunnel, but in reality the passage from integration project mode to 'business as usual' is a gradual one; there is no specific moment where one can confidently say, "job done". In the absence of some signal that is given to mark the end of the integration project and the beginning of the next chapter of the company's existence, the integration process will appear endless, with a constant flow of new tasks and topics that need addressing – it will feel like running up a downward moving escalator...

As organisations are constantly adapting to their environment and anticipating future challenges, waiting for the company to have truly *stabilised* before declaring the end of the integration process is illusory. As discussed earlier, once the integrated organisations has reached the crucial stage of presenting 'one face to the customer', there is still plenty of work to do, less urgent but equally important, until the two constituent companies have fully blended into one another. Rather than waiting until some kind of 'end state' is reached, focusing instead on the completion of a few key milestones will make more sense. These will be, in most cases, 'people related' because this is what affects the staff's life – the completion of the resourcing process, office moves, possibly the closing-down of some factories, warehouses or sales outlets. The fact that information systems might not be fully integrated by then, or that the supply chain and manufacturing footprint are not yet seamless between the two former organisations probably matters less, because these are part of adjustments that are often an on-going process in business life. The key advantage of making this arbitrary cut is that it can in almost all cases be made within 12 months after Day One. Psychologically, for most people, that one-year limit marks the distinction between transient phases of business life and the more permanent state of things. More than 12 months and everything appears to be dragging on endlessly.

Getting closure on the integration process is particularly important because in the process of a merger or the absorption of a major acquisition, it is easy for companies to become very inwardly focused as they try to sort themselves out, learn to work together and resolve unforeseen problems and issues as they occur. Even when the basic rule is applied of allocating individuals to the project and others to the daily business, the integration that is taking place in the background is a source of uncertainty and worries for most people, which makes them think about themselves rather than about the imperatives of the business. The sooner the customers and the company's products or services can return to the centre of the radar screen, the better.

Celebrating success

Achieving a successful integration is cause for celebration. As the cost of the integration is likely to have ended up being higher than initially anticipated – remember the comments made in chapters 6 and 9 – there probably will not be much of a budget for eccentric festivities at the end of the programme. The objective here is not for the celebration to be sumptuous, but for the moment to be festive, because it marks an accomplishment, and joyous, because the future is brighter now the two organisations have joined forces. It acknowledges the efforts of everyone in the organisation in either integrating the company or keeping the daily business on track, and pays tribute to a few 'heroes' for their special contribution.

As mentioned earlier, celebrating success on several occasions when key integration milestones are reached is important, to maintain momentum and acknowledge that people's inordinate efforts are not being taken for granted. But the 'End of Integration' celebration is more than this. It is the closure of one chapter of the company's history, and the beginning of a new era. It will also be the time to introduce new initiatives that follow on from the integration. These will mostly be concerned with the *transformation* of the organisation that, after having reached some stability and organisational coherence, needs to prepare to tackle the next challenges of the future. Whatever balance the company will have decided to strike between the non-negotiable imperatives of integration and its desire to create a paradigm shift by transforming its culture and ways of working, anything that could not be achieved during the integration phase will need to be tackled right afterwards. The End of Integration celebration is the ideal moment to acknowledge achievements to date, and spell out what is next on the menu. This is all about ensuring that the organisation does not fall into the trap of remaining inwardly focused, and that all the people in the company begin to look forwards again, into the future, towards new common objectives.

Redeployment

This project is over – what about the next one?

When the integration project team was being pulled together, one of the key concerns was to plan how these individuals would redeploy into the business, safeguarding the knowledge they have accumulated during this quite unique experience. Now is the time to start putting these redeployment plans into action. The process is likely to be gradual; some initiatives will still be on going when the integration project is officially announced as completed, and therefore in most cases the project team will dissolve gradually into the organisation rather than being disbanded in one step.

The *transformation* projects or other similar initiatives on which the company is likely to embark after the integration phase will also require project team members. The temptation will be to keep the same individuals, because with the experience of the integration project they will almost certainly fit all the criteria: familiarity with the imperatives of project work, broad business knowledge, flexibility, mobility, self-motivation – the list of positive attributes is long.

Every company, particularly large organisations, has a few 'project animals': individuals who thrive on project work, who enjoy the diversity and intensity of projects, and for whom being in a 'real job' is tantamount to boredom. They might always have been 'project animals', or discovered this trait in themselves while on the integration programme. Great! There is still a lot to do in an organisation that has just recently integrated and these individuals will be immensely valuable. For the others, one would be well advised to think very hard before re-appointing members of the integration team to the project teams of the other initiatives that are about to commence, for the following reasons:

▪ When appointing individuals to the integration project team, some commitment may have been made regarding people's redeployment at the close of the project and it is imperative that such commitments be honoured, failing which it will not be possible to adequately resource any significant projects in the future.

▪ The members of the integration project team are 'super-users' in their respective fields, with an in-depth knowledge of their function with the added benefit of understanding better than most people within the organisation how their function relates to others. This is because a lot of the integration work will have been concerned with harmonising processes that flow across functions. Re-deploying these individuals into the organisation ensures that help and support is at hand for other staff who might feel a little disoriented during the early months of the post-integration era, and that the broader vision and understanding of the integration project team members spreads to their other colleagues over time.

■ Pulling staff off their daily job to join a project team is effective when the project lasts up to one, or possibly two years, but after that length of time there is a definite risk that the daily business will have evolved to an extent such that these long-standing project team members begin to be cut off from the reality of the business and gradually become akin to consultants or contractors, rather than representatives and champions of the business.

■ There is one additional reason for wanting to rotate the staff appointed to projects, which I believe to be up to the company's discretion, depending on the style it wishes to adopt. In many companies, 'project work' is viewed as a curse, a sidetrack, the possible end of career progression. 'Projects' are where people disappear from the radar screen, where they get forgotten and one day drop out of the organisation because at some point there are no more projects to be delivered.

Even in companies where this is not the case there is always some degree of fear of project work. This is why staffing large project teams, such as those required for a company integration or other significant initiatives such as an ERP replacement, is always such a difficult and tedious task. Successfully redeploying the project team that served on the integration and recruiting other individuals to tackle the next initiatives is a powerful way of signalling that project work is part of the company's culture, that project work is a very effective development tool, and that individuals are expected at some point to serve on a project as part of their own career path. This is not only very enriching for the staff community in general, but also ensures that over time each project or major initiative is supported by the talent of the most appropriate individuals because they will aspire to that experience rather than fear it.

Knowledge retention

The value of retaining the knowledge that accumulated during the integration process is evident. *How* to go about retaining this knowledge is another matter. This is why I recommended that thoughts about how individuals will be redeployed into the organisation must be an integral part of the project team resourcing process itself – failure to do so will leave senior management with a serious problem when the integration is completed.

The corollary of this is that the names, skills, experience and other attributes of the integration project team members must be documented and be highly visible when the company's structure is being designed and when the appointments to that new structure are being planned (see chapter 4). In many cases, the integration project team members will not be in a position to be released back to the business soon enough, and some work-around will be needed to fill in those temporary vacancies, but the key aim must be to avoid losing members of the integration team because you have not been able to redeploy them in a timely manner.

One of the key factors that can cause a member of the integration project team to be 'forgotten' in the resourcing process of the organisation is that his or her line-manager, who initially freed that individual to join the project team, is no longer in the integrated post-merger structure. When people are appointed to a project of this magnitude, they need at least two 'sponsors'. Their initial line-manager would naturally be the first one, but as the organisation is about to undergo a complete transformation, it is advisable that each member of the integration project team be linked to one member of the project's Steering Committee, who will have the ultimate responsibility to ensure a successful redeployment into the business when the integration programme reaches completion.

> *Thoughts about how individuals will be redeployed into the organisation at the end of the project must be an integral part of the initial project team resourcing process*

Looking forwards, not inwardly

New focus for senior management

"Phew, it's over" is probably what many senior managers will be thinking while raising a toast to the successful integration during the celebration party. The intensity and duration of the integration process is such that not having something momentous to follow on afterwards is likely to cause a sensation of anti-climax, a general drop in energy and, more importantly, the very dangerous feeling throughout the organisation that the company has reached its end destination, rather than merely an important milestone of an on-going journey.

Maintaining the impetus and energy, and avoiding the emergence of a sense of self-gratification is crucial. Now that the scale of the organisation has significantly increased and the effectiveness of its processes has improved as a result of the integration process, it is vital to capitalize on these strengths and reap the benefits of this competitive advantage, because these were a key component of the benefits case that had initially led to the decision to proceed with the merger or acquisition.

For the members of the Executive, painting a vivid picture of this mid-term future is a key responsibility. This is all about harnessing the energy that will have built up during the integration process, and projecting it towards the future – not the long-term vision that was part of the justification for the integration, but something more accessible, something closer: i.e. what needs to be accomplished within the next twelve to eighteen months.

At the celebration event marking the end of the integration project, people were looking at each other, congratulating everyone for a job well done. From that moment onwards, the task is to get people to stop looking at each other, inwardly, and instead to start looking together in one same direction towards the next challenge and major milestone that will have been defined by the Executive team.

Defining the future focus

Defining that next big goal, the major milestone on the journey towards the Company's vision, is almost as complex as the whole communication exercise that took place when the decision to merge or make that major acquisition was announced. Looking at a timeline, the key elements of that next big step need to be articulated very clearly by the Executive three to six months before the anticipated date of the End of Integration, as it will take that much time to understand the implications for the various groups of stakeholders and develop compelling communication messages for each of these audiences.

At this point of the integration, most people in the company – from the Executive to middle management and down to the shop floor – are likely to feel worn out by the intensity and pace of what they have lived through. The responsibility of the Executive team is to remember that integrating the two companies was just an initial step that would enable a much greater scheme to take place. Companies do not become more successful just by becoming larger – they need to do things in a very different way that will surpass their competitors and attract new customers. From the point of view of the Executive Team, successfully managing the integration is just a means for that greater objective. And striving for that objective begins now: when the integration is completed. Therefore defining what the next steps will be is not a secondary task; it is at the very core of the plan that makes two companies join forces to tackle the market in an unprecedented way, the realisation of the synergies that were promised in the merger or acquisition's business case.

> *Companies do not become more successful just by becoming larger – they need to do things in a very different way that will surpass their competitors and attract new customers.*

The next steps

Post-implementation review

Regardless of whether the company is on a regular acquisition trail or whether the integration that has just been completed feels like a once-in-a-generation event, a thorough review of what has been achieved is an absolute necessity. This is the right time to evaluate whether the savings, efficiency improvements and other synergies that were promised in the business case have been realised, and decide on corrective action, if necessary, and add this to the list of outstanding activities. Although the integration has officially been declared as 'done', there are inevitably ramifications of integration activities that extend beyond the official end of the project.

This is when the integration project's Steering Committee must stand up to its accountability for the outcome of the integration. The Post-Implementation Review measures the extent to which the vision that was painted when the acquisition or merger was decided has translated into a reality, and is thereby the formal appraisal of the Steering Committee's success. Once the Post-Implementation Review is completed, the company switches from being predominantly in 'project mode' to being 'business as usual' and the Steering Committee can adjourn because it has finished its mission.

While the celebration that takes place at the end of the integration process marks the beginning of a new chapter for the staff across the whole company, the Post-Implementation Review is the formal rite of passage that discharges the members of the Steering Committee from their former responsibilities on the project and establishes an orderly catalogue of what has yet to be implemented – the key here is to make sure that nothing falls through the net.

Lessons learnt

No matter how well the integration process took place, as a result of careful planning, strong project management and a combination of favourable elements (a bit of luck always helps, even in the best managed projects!), as one might expect in every project, there are always some aspects that could have been planned or managed even better, as well as some that might have run smoother than expected and from which lessons can be learnt.

When reaching the end of a marathon project such as an integration, most people are glad to return to daily business, with a mix of fond and less pleasurable memories of this very unique experience. Unless this knowledge and understanding of what went well or less well is captured in a structured manner, its value will be lost to the company as people move on to other jobs, change departments, leave the company over the years or otherwise forget about some of the factors that triggered specific events or outcomes during the integration process.

Reviewing 'lessons learnt' as part of the post-implementation review is therefore a valuable exercise provided the company refers to this document the next time a project of any particular significance is about to be undertaken in the future. Lessons learnt only make sense if they are *applied* subsequently, rather than just sitting in a file. This appears as a truism, and yet when companies embark on an integration programme, many of them run into difficulties for not having taken sufficient notice of advice given to them by consultants or other such specialists, which are based on benchmarks and the past experience of other companies. Ambitious 'hungry' managers tend to think that they can systematically outperform the market's benchmarks and so end up under-estimating the resources or time-scales required to perform certain integration tasks. Being able to refer to lessons learnt documented on the basis of the company's own history is more compelling than external benchmarks – they are a reality check, the statement of how things have worked in one's own business, rather than a sample of supposedly similar companies, and as such can be immensely helpful in ensuring that the company really engages in a learning curve that will significantly enhance its future capability to tackle broadscale initiatives and complex projects.

As a rough guide, the areas that would (as a minimum) typically be covered in the 'lessons learnt' review and document are the following:

1. Due diligence: with the benefit of hindsight, and given the specificities of our type of business, are there areas that should have been investigated more thoroughly prior to finalising the acquisition papers or merger documents?

2. How well were synergies and savings estimated in the original business case, both in terms of their magnitude and their timing? What were the key factors or decisions that lead to significant over- or under-estimates?

3. How realistic were the timings set in the integration plan?

4. How realistic was the resource plan for the integration team? (Under this heading, consider in more detail the functions related to Finance and Human Resources)

5. How effective was the resourcing process of the integration team?

6. How effective has the redeployment of that team been so far? How actively was redeployment being planned during the course of the project?

7. What were the key elements that safeguarded business performance during the integration process, or, conversely, what that damaged business performance?

8. Looking at the integration timeline, how appropriate was the speed of the integration process (the balance between 'fit for purpose' versus 'search of world class excellence')

9. How efficiently were external resources (contractors and consultants) used and what could be improved?

10. How well were industrial relations managed and what can we learn from that?

11. How effective was the programme governance and internal organisation? Did we struggle to reach agreement on key decisions or resolve important issues?

12. What specific behaviours displayed by the Executive, senior management, middle management and team leaders helped or otherwise distracted the integration process?

13. How effective were the communications during the integration? (Frequency, consistency, reach, clarity, format and channels, languages)

Including the feedback of others

At the end of a long voyage such as a company integration, any seasoned programme director will have a personal opinion of what went well or could have gone better. Others might have a different perspective, and some individuals may have experienced some aspects of the integration that might appear to have run smoothly as a particularly challenging or harsh phase of the project. Gathering feedback from the members of the integration project team and from the Steering Committee as well as from a sample of people across the organisation will give a more holistic dimension to the review process; it is also the best means of ensuring that the people to whom the review will be presented identify with its findings and conclusions, and therefore that the 'lessons learnt' have a better chance of being applied in the future.

Allowing time for debate

To be meaningful, the gathering and summarising of lessons learnt is a time consuming exercise because it requires the analysis of substantial volumes of data, feedback from individuals, the review of minutes and reports, a thorough read through the Issues Log, the Stakeholder Management notes, and the documents relating to Risk Management. As mentioned earlier, when the integration process has reached the stage of presenting 'One Face to the Customer' and can be considered as essentially complete (at least for the outside world), a number of strands of the programme still need to be brought to completion, some of them may be extremely complex. This is the right moment to make the Executive of the Company aware of what can be organised or structured in a more efficient manner to run major initiatives in a smoother manner from now on.

When the 'lessons learnt' review document is ready, the learning opportunity can be maximised by circulating the document to the members of the Executive well in advance of the review session, and really engaging in debate about some of the key points. The outcome of such a review should not be only to take note of what could have been done better, but actually to commit or at least agree on how differently things will be tackled when the next big initiative is undertaken. That next big initiative might not be that far away: once organisations have integrated the basic elements of their core processes, have reached a degree of newly-found stability and can present 'One Face to the Customer', the next step they need to envisage is an in-depth integration of their Information Systems which, in the easiest instance, calls for the extension of the system running in one of the former companies to include the newly-integrated business or, in the more challenging scenario, for a complete ERP replacement.

A daunting prospect, but the learning derived from the experience of the integration programme will be immensely valuable, and the time invested in gathering and analysing the feedback from the integration team members and evaluating the outcomes of each key stage of the integration programme will have been well invested.

Avoiding orphans at the 'End of Integration'

The official end of a significant project is greeted with a sense of celebration, but also with a sigh of relief. But that *"phew, we did it!"* feeling must not obscure the fact that some non-essential elements of the integration work may not yet have been completed.

One very important element during the wrap-up is therefore to run through the list of 'open items' and agree a clear way forward for each of them. These are pieces of unfinished work, possibly a number of items that at the 'official' end of the programme had not yet satisfied all the acceptance criteria and therefore require some rework. Whatever these are, they are deliverables that do not compromise the desired outcome of the programme or cause significant dysfunction and therefore do not justify maintaining a programme Steering Board to oversee their execution, but nonetheless they cannot be left to fall by the wayside and be forgotten, and therefore a formal decision is needed for each of these.

In some instances, the value of completing a piece of unfinished work may not be deemed to be worth the time, effort or cost involved. People often struggle to scrap something that has been started but not completed, because this acknowledges a waste of the resources and effort invested thus far. A waste it might be, but that waste is a sunk cost, and what really matters is whether there still is a valid 'mini-business-case' that justifies completing that open item. Quite often, one may find that the very reason that these items were not completed is that the people involved had sensed it was not a huge priority and focused their attention to other more crucial aspects of the integration. There is nothing embarrassing about culling sub-projects that might have been viewed as necessary when the integration was started: developments during the course of the integration may result in situations that reduce the need or value of some of the project's initial deliverables. This applies, of course, to the implementation of work initiated by contingency plans, which is no longer needed but which tends to get a life of its own in large organisations. However, inevitably there will also be many other deliverables that one might be able to do without, simply because things have moved on in the company... Ruthlessly asking the question *"Do we really need this?"* is therefore a necessary step that will reduce clutter in the organisation: now that the integration project is essentially complete, the company will need to refocus its energy on other pursuits.

Once the integration project's Steering Board and the company's Executive have reached agreement on which open items are worth completing, responsibility for bringing these to a close therefore rests with the company's Executive, or individuals nominated by them, to be resolved in the course of normal daily business. At this point, the Steering Board has completed its mission and can be dissolved. Consequently, the only way to ensure that the last remaining open items of the integration programme do not conveniently fall into oblivion is to dedicate one point of the Executive's regular meeting agenda to a quick but formal review of progress achieved on completing the integration's open items until each of them has been nailed down.

Preserving unity

After the strain and efforts deployed during a number of months to integrate two companies, it will always be tempting to relax a little, enjoy what has been accomplished, and assume far too early that the newly-formed company has reached a steady state. This is usually not the case, for a number of reasons, and unless further efforts and specific actions are undertaken there is a serious risk that centrifugal forces will appear to undermine the recently developed feeling of unity.

What causes these centrifugal forces? Quite simply anything that prevents the company from running smoothly and which may, rightly or wrongly, be attributed to the integration. The business integration is seen as the culprit because the two organisations that have just merged didn't appear to suffer from those same problems when the two companies were still distinct entities. Such problems can appear several months after the integration's 'official' completion: they are not necessarily the consequence of a job half-done, but rather of poor training or the lack of solid temporary processes to bridge the period until every aspect of the integration has been fully implemented, including Manufacturing, the Supply Chain and the company's Information Systems.

One of the usual suspects is data management. Invariably when companies merge, they realise the extent to which their internal data was either incomplete or slightly corrupt. In a steady state, the adverse consequence of poor data can be contained because the individuals working in the organisation usually have the knowledge and awareness needed to fill the gaps or overcome the issues arising from poor or missing data. This is no longer the case once the company has undergone a thorough transformation. Data cleansing is a lengthy and sometimes tedious exercise. It is seldom completed by the time two companies are theoretically ready to operate as one. However, not only should the data cleansing exercise be completed rigorously, but processes and accountabilities need to be defined to ensure that thorough data management will continue as an on-going discipline in the merged company. This is too often overlooked. Data management is not sexy and is not usually perceived as a high value-added activity. And yet in the context of the integration of two organisations one needs to be aware that issues arising from data will inevitably crystallise the divide between the two companies one is painstakingly trying to unite.

Everything can appear to be functioning well in the early months following the integration because vigilance levels are high, things get double-checked to prevent errors, and the feeling of excitement that follows the integration makes up for the fatigue most people will have accumulated during the merger. Data issues may take a while to reveal the full extent of their significance and ugliness.

I have seen cases in which missing or incomplete data caused errors in the supply chain between the two former companies, resulting in the wrong product being delivered or unacceptably long delays in product availability. Having spent time and effort developing and delivering product training to the sales teams of both former companies, the salesmen reverted to selling exclusively the products of their pre-merger range because these were the ones they could be sure of obtaining on time and in full from the factories, whereas the 'other range' had been a source of repeated problems that undermined their relationship with their customers. Small cause – big consequences resulting in significant missed opportunities. With its sales forces across Europe focusing on the products they knew from the past rather than offering its new comprehensive range, this company failed for a whole year to capture one of the key elements of the merger's benefits case. It took no time at all for people in the whole organisation to switch back to referring to the products as the range from company A and the range from company B, effectively shifting people's hearts and minds back by 18 months to the days when the integration was about to begin...

Badly stored mayonnaise can curdle. So can integrated companies if a conscious effort is not deployed systematically during the first two years of their new existence to continuously reinforce the cement that holds the organisation together, and address as a matter of high priority any issues that can be a cause of division.

Creating a new organisation from the basis of two companies that have decided to join their destiny is an exciting project that can capture people's imagination and mobilize their energy. Repairing something that has failed is a far less inspiring venture: it will take inordinate amounts of energy, communication and persuasion to overcome the cynicism and scepticism that develop in organisations when 'the merger hasn't worked'. It is therefore the responsibility of the company's Executive to ensure that post-integration activities are followed-up and that a mechanism is in place to rapidly resolve any issues that may arise while the company is still progressing on its learning curve and getting to grips with what it means to be 'one organisation'.

> *The only way to ensure that the last remaining open items of the integration programme do not conveniently fall into oblivion is to dedicate one point of the Executive's regular meeting agenda to a quick but formal review of progress achieved on completing the integration's open items, until each of them has been nailed down.*

When all is done and dusted...

Statistics on the percentage of mergers that can be considered a success vary greatly depending on the source, possibly because of the diverse ways of defining success. In the introduction to this book, I spelt out my definition as being the completion of the integration process in full, on time and within budget, and the realisation of the business case, or at least of the organisation capable of delivering it. This is because the focus of this book is on how to make the integration happen without damaging the dynamics of the on-going business, and therefore allow the merger or acquisition's business case to be realised.

I started this book comparing the merger of two organisations with making a perfect mayonnaise. This was not formulating an opinion as to whether mayonnaise is a good thing, whether it is healthy, but more about ensuring that separate ingredients blend into something smooth and homogenous. Botch the integration of the companies and it will not be worth wondering whether the merger or acquisition was a good idea to begin with! The best business case will not materialise if poorly executed.

Nonetheless, when it comes to overall lessons learnt, the real 'proof of the pudding' comes a little later, and warrants some analysis and debate respectively one and two years after the official end of the integration programme, and this is for two reasons:

▊ Even if the integration was run smoothly, it is only after a year, possibly two years, that the business case that led to the acquisition or merger can truly be verified:

○ Were all the synergies realised?

○ Is the combined business growing faster than it would have if the companies had remained apart?

○ Have the business's strengths and opportunities improved and provided the company with an enhanced competitive and strategic advantage?

○ Do the company's Key Performance Indicators support the notion that the business is not only *larger*, but actually *better*?

While there is possibly not much the company can do about some of the above points after the event, they provide valuable learning for future acquisitions or other such business expansion ventures. Getting a feel for aspects that might have been under-estimated in the original business case generates corporate wisdom and the ability to set up better deals in the future.

▌ The second test one and two years down the road after the official end of the integration programme is concerned with how well the two organisations have actually 'gelled' together:

○ Can we detect any reversal trends towards the separate former values of the two constituent companies?

○ Do employees still see themselves as "ex-company A" and "ex-company B" staff; do they still tend to refer to "we" and "they"?

○ Have the results of the staff surveys evolved positively since the early days of the integration process? Do staff feel that promises have been kept and honoured?

○ Do the staff believe that the new integrated company is a better one than either of the two former organisations?

This last point is probably the strongest driver of cohesion or division within the integration organisation: any feelings that the former companies were 'better' – as subjective as that may be – are likely to promote a reversal of behaviours and ways of working that can cause the company to become quite dysfunctional.

Importantly, and in contrast to the lessons that can be learnt from the post-event evaluation of the integration's business case, the findings relating to how well the two organisations have gelled not only provide learnings for future acquisitions or mergers, but can and should be acted upon: if the observed outcome does not match initial expectations, it is not too late to do something about it. Early signs of a reversal into former behaviour patterns and a dilution of the sense of common identify should not be accepted as an inevitability. The main element that needs to be remembered here is that the values and behaviours that are promoted during the integration process take time to really become engrained in the daily life of an organisation; they need to undergo some form of reality check in the company before they can really be considered as *assimilated*. Conversely, they can become irrelevant if developments and circumstances in the early years that follow the merger put these values and behaviours at odds with what the individuals working in the organisation can observe in daily business life.

The above is not based on hard facts or numbers, but relates rather to a possible mismatch between individuals' expectations and the actual outcome of the integration process, hence the importance of conducting employee surveys even in the very early stages of the integration. By doing so, one can observe the evolution of the staff's perceptions, concerns and expectations as they evolve along the curve of change acceptance that normally occurs in such circumstances. When the initial survey is conducted, before the integration activity actually commences, most people in the organisation may already be in a mood of denial or scepticism.

> *It is the soft factors such as the sense of company identity, commitment and energy levels of the management and staff, which will determine the organisation's ability to operate as one.*

Many models of organisational change concur to show how morale takes a deep dip as a result of rejection before understanding can lead to gradual acceptance and, as individuals perceive and comprehend the benefits of the change, to commitment. It is crucial to take the pulse of the organisation one year and two years after the integration has taken place, to confirm that this commitment is still there, and react if the early signs of any deterioration are perceived. In particular, companies that are on an acquisition trail, or operating in an industry that is undergoing a significant consolidation phase, cannot afford to contemplate their next merger or significant acquisition until they have sufficiently digested the one they have just lived through.

Once all the technical aspects and processes are harmonised in a merged company, when the manufacturing footprint, supply chain, portfolio rationalisation, organisation and office locations have been redesigned and implemented, it is the soft factors such as the sense of company identity, commitment and energy levels of the management and staff, that will determine the organisation's ability to operate as one, to fully live the business case that had prompted the integration, to single-mindedly set out to beat the competition, and possibly to be poised for the next quantum leap: another major acquisition or joining forces with another company.

Now it's your turn!

Throughout this book, I have focused on the *approach* to integrating organisations, rather than the *content* of the integration process.

The *content* will be dependent on the type of business and sector of activity, and my assumption is that the people at the helm of the companies that are about to integrate have in-depth knowledge of their business sector. Furthermore, when it comes to running in-depth analyses of the companies' processes, manufacturing or supply chain efficiencies, remuneration and reward schemes, technical infrastructure and other such specialised areas, every large international company and most medium-sized businesses are likely to need the input and support of external consultants. Those consultants bring expert knowledge to the table, as well as industry benchmarks that are key in setting the levels of excellence towards which the future integrated company will want to strive. The content describes what needs to be analysed, decided and implemented to reach the desired 'end-state' of the integration.

The *approach*, on the other hand, is about the *journey* that will get you there. It is less than an exact science as I attempted to illustrate throughout this book. Whereas the content is concerned with the 'what', which can result from rigorous analysis, the approach is about choosing the 'how' and the 'why': it is the result of deliberate decisions by senior management for which they will be held accountable.

Most mergers or acquisition integrations fail because senior management have underestimated the complexity and magnitude of the task, very often as a result of discounting the recommendations and warnings provided to them by their auditors or other external consultants. "Surely it needn't be that complicated". "This is overkill: we can do it faster and cheaper". "People in this company are used to change and won't struggle with this one either". "Of course they're trying to send us an army of consultants and charge us a fortune".

Clearly, assisting the integration of two sizeable companies is good business for business consultants, and it is right that one should challenge how much support is actually needed. Nonetheless, I hope in this book to have highlighted in a more tangible way the crucial areas of the integration voyage that require particular care and rigour, and the potential consequences of 'cutting corners'. Ultimately, where a company sets the bar will depend on its attitude to risk, possible prior experience with acquisitions and mergers, and what it can afford to invest in the integration.

For any business integration involving a certain degree of complexity and/or geographical spread, there are still a few key principles that I passionately believe cannot suffer any compromise:

- Clarity of intent:

  - Re-think the merger or acquisition's business case to make it relevant to each of the stakeholder groups who will be impacted: this includes all levels of staff.

  - Repeat and reinforce the messages continuously, or else they will get distorted over time.

- Segregation of duties:

  - Appoint someone to the Executive team as Integration Director to focus *solely* on the integration; bring in an experienced interim executive for this task if no suitable candidate is available internally: do not expect the CEO, CFO or HR director to take on this role in addition to their on-going responsibilities in the business.

  - Set-up a 'ring-fenced' team in charge of the integration; allow the rest of the organisation to focus on 'business as usual' and delivering the budgeted profit: any shortfall in on-going commercial results will derail the integration process.

- Organisation and accountability:

  - Strive to get the best, brightest and most innovative people onto the integration team; beware of candidates that are too easily available!

  - Agree from the onset of the integration project the principles that will govern the redeployment of the project team upon completion, and ensure those principles are transparent and well communicated to all the team members.

  - Organise the integration project members in outcome-based teams to ensure good cross-functional interaction and generate solutions that consider all aspects of the business.

○ Remember that a lot of pre-work can take place before Day One: ensure clear communication and understanding of the legal restrictions that apply, and strive to get as much pre-work and data gathering done within the limits set by legislation.

■ Leadership and personal impact:

○ Before the start of the integration, think about what you need to do or change to withstand the forthcoming prolonged work pressure (sport, diet, 'me-time').

○ Run through the list of general success factors and temperament attributes, identify your strengths and weaknesses, make yourself repeatedly aware of your strengths and how you can best use them during the integration; address critical weaknesses (train, nominate a coach or feedback-buddy).

○ Remember to remain visible, approachable and open to dialogue; remain acutely aware of your body language.

○ Do not assume that people will ask the burning questions that are on their minds: ensure a 'safe' onvironmont is croatod to oncourago dialoguo on thoso issues, alleviate anxieties, promote understanding and acceptance of change.

■ Communication

○ Beyond the question of what budget is being set aside, have you realistically allowed sufficient *time* and resource for communication?

○ Use several channels to reinforce coherence and ensure all audiences are reached.

○ Do not craft 'one size fits all' communications: adapt to the variety of audiences to ensure relevance and understanding.

○ Remember that multi-lingual communication may require two and a half to three times longer to produce than single version documents.

None of the above should come as a surprise; most of this is pure common sense. Running through checklists from time to time to ensure that good practice is in place and continues to be observed will help keep the integration on track. The key difficulty relates to the need to be aware of one's leadership style, to control it and maintain high levels of personal energy. For some people this will come quite naturally, for others it will require a conscious effort that might become a serious challenge as stress levels rise and fatigue sets in after months of continuous intense work pressure and relative uncertainty.

The size of the task should not be daunting, because good preparation will ensure you will be in a position to master it, having realistically assessed the time and resources that will be required and planned what it will take for yourself, the integration team and the rest of the company's staff to manage the pressure and deliver outstanding results.

With the immensely fulfilling achievement of being among the 20% of companies that really got it right.

> *Most mergers or acquisition integrations fail because senior management have underestimated the complexity and magnitude of the task, very often as a result of discounting the recommendations and warnings that were provided to them.*

In Essence...

▊ *At some arbitrary point in time, after achieving 'One Face to the Customer', the integration must be declared complete, even though some ramifications of the integration will stretch over months beyond that date.*

▊ *Getting closure on the integration allows the organisation to focus again wholly on driving the day-to-day business, to look forwards rather than inwardly, and aim for its next big challenge.*

▊ *That 'next big challenge' must be thought through by the Executive well in advance of the 'End of Integration' to maintain momentum and build on the energy developed during the integration phase.*

▊ *Redeploying the members of the integration project team into the business is key to retain crucial knowledge, and to benefit from their role as super-users who can help their colleagues in getting familiar with the company's new processes and ways of working.*

▊ *A post-implementation review must take place to assess whether the business case has been realised, whether the savings and efficiency improvements have materialised, and decide on corrective action if necessary.*

▊ *A formal review of lessons learnt during the integration will provide invaluable information for future large scale initiatives ... or the next acquisition.*

▊ *Any remaining 'open items' of the project must be reviewed in terms of their relevance ("do we really need this?") and priority; those that need to be implemented must be given an 'owner' and be followed up as an additional agenda items during the regular meetings of the Executive.*

■ *Conduct a survey of the staff's perceptions, concerns and expectations one and two years after the end of the project, to ascertain that centrifugal forces are not undermining the unity you crafted during the integration phase.*

Appendix

Pre-integration preparation activities

The headings below provide a structured checklist of the integration-related activities that can take place at various stages of the integration process.

Preparation during due diligence

A thorough due diligence will have looked at all relevant aspects that may potentially reduce the value of the company that is being acquired or is candidate to a merger. However, in preparation for the *integration* and bearing in mind that most integrations lead to significant organisation change, the following additional topics need particular attention as they impact the *duration and the cost of the integration*, rather than the *intrinsic value* of the two companies in their present state:

▮ Agreement on the type of data that will be shared before the two companies are legally under common ownership (within the limits of the relevant legislations on competition) as well as data that will be made available under confidentiality clauses to third parties for the purpose of pre-merger analysis.

▮ Check on data completeness and accuracy relating to the information that will be exchanged.

▮ Review by third-party of contracts of senior personnel to identify 'golden parachutes', discrepancies between current role and reporting lines in the organisation and those contained in the contracts.

∎ History of social plans and other precedents relating to Human Resources.

If any factors are identified from the above list that are likely to significantly impact the duration or cost of the integration, these need to be flagged very clearly so as to manage expectations when the decision is made to proceed with the acquisition or merger.

List of imperative preparation before Day One

There is a long raft of actions that need to take place either before the legal acquisition or merger transaction can become effective, or immediately on the first day of common ownership for the transaction to take full legal effect. It is essential that this list be comprehensive, with a clear indication of who will do what on Day One and a briefing to those responsible for carrying out the tasks to ensure an orderly execution. The areas affected will depend on the type of business, but would include as a minimum:

∎ Company and Project governance

○ Appointment of Board of Directors.

○ Appointment of the Executive; as a minimum this must include the CEO, the head of Finance and the head of HR. Other roles may be appointed subsequently after Day One.

○ Appointment of non-executive Directors, arrangements for resignation of the leavers from the former constituent companies.

○ Appointment of integrated company's auditors.

◯ Constitution of the integration project's Steering Board: appointment of the Programme Director in charge of the integration and all subsequent activities relating to the design of the programme organisation structure, appointment of team members (at least for the key roles), establish rules and procedures relating to the project's management, systems, project logistics, HR support and 'house rules' for project work stream members.

▌ Legal & Business Continuity:

◯ Regulatory clearance of new company, changes relating to registered offices.

◯ Government undertakings, if relevant.

◯ New company name and corporate identity (final or provisional).

◯ Legal completion of the transaction: ensure that all conditions of the agreements arc met and if not, draft a letter covering those conditions that have not been met.

◯ Ensure all third party consents required by the agreement are secured (this can relate to suppliers, distributors, licences including software usage rights, and more generally to all contracts and agreements that contain a change of control clause).

◯ Prepare for recognition of the new legal entity with authorities and administration (e.g. import/export documents, excise authorities, VAT.

◯ Inform relevant authorities of change in ownership of intellectual property rights, patents, trademarks; and secure all usage for all existing and new brands, names and trademarks.

○ Manage continuity of services provided by a parent company or other business unit (in the case of a company acquired from another group).

○ Ensure continuity of contracts relating to suppliers of goods and services and other external parties; secure transfer of external leases from prior owners.

○ List of contracts currently under negotiation and relevant action points for execution immediately after the legal transaction has taken place.

○ Prepare banking arrangements ready for Day One.

○ Establish the provisional reporting lines by business and geography that will apply from Day One onwards, until the target organisation is set up.

○ Continuity of all insurance covers, either through existing insurance policies or new ones.

○ Asset valuation and stock count (or stock reconciliation if not performed on Day One).

○ Establish that there is no deterioration in the credit ratings or creditworthiness of the legacy organisations (to prevent any 'events of default' from being triggered under debt agreements or credit limits with suppliers).

■ Organisation Readiness

○ Establish and communicate the provisional reporting

lines by business and geography that will apply from Day One onwards, until the target organisation is set up.

○ Verify and plan staff transfer procedures. In the United Kingdom, check that no TUPE (Transfer of Undertakings Protection of Employment) protected transfers will take place on Day One or document those that do and identify any subsequent transfers where TUPE will apply. Restrictions of a similar nature exist in the employment legislation of many other countries.

○ Draft new employment contract letters also covering issues such as status of eligibility and continuation of pension policy.

○ Define signature rights and authority limits; ensure these are aligned with the hierarchical levels and roles currently existing in the two companies to avoid any possible misinterpretation from Day One onwards.

■ Communications

○ Preparation of communication for Day One (communication plan and full content) for internal and external parties (e.g. website, employee welcome pack, customer pack, supplier pack, media pack, press releases, press conference as appropriate).

Additional preparation during regulatory approval process

Once the due diligence process is completed and the decision to merge or acquire a company has been made, the time that elapses between that decision and the receipt of the required authorisations to proceed can be put to good use: good preparation allows the integration to commence swiftly as soon as all the authorisations have been received. In the case of international mergers, clearance to merge or acquire is needed from several regulatory bodies and the overall process can therefore last a number of months; typically two to six months depending on the complexity of the business and its competitive environment.

Gathering all the data that will be required for the integration process, ensuring its completeness and coherence and converting it to agreed standardised formats that will facilitate comparisons and analysis, is a resource- and time-consuming task. The more such preparation can take place before Day One, the better equipped the integration teams will be to kick-off the integration to a head start.

In addition to the gathering of data, in some cases it may be possible for an independent third-party bound by confidentiality clauses to pre-analyse some of the data provided by the two merging organisations. This can include information that competition law would not allow the two companies to share directly.

As the delineation between the type of information that can or cannot be shared can, in some instances, result from subtle interpretations of competition law, it is wise to tread with caution and base those decisions on legal advice from well-informed practitioners, and to document precisely what information has been shared and discussed and what topics were deliberately not covered. Employees and managers involved in these data gathering exercises prior to Day One need to be made aware of the legal restrictions that apply to their task. When the information gathering requires a project team to assemble in a workshop or group discussion, it is advisable to include the presence of an independent legal counsel who can provide a steer as to what may or may not be discussed, and who will certify that the meeting complied with the restrictions imposed by the applicable legislation. Such documentation is valuable in the event that the regulatory authorities, or a competitor, or any other external stakeholder, were to challenge the way the integration is being prepared or accuse the companies of being in breach of the legislation.

Examples of the type of preparation work that is not essential for Day One but can greatly accelerate the integration thereafter include the following:

Finance

▮ Preparation for the alignment of the accounting structures: cost and profit centre definitions, account definitions and structures, documentation of accounting practices and methods used for cost calculations. In some cases, it may be possible to set up the overall accounting structure ahead of Day One.

▮ Transition plan towards common accounting periods if the two companies' accounting is based on different bases (e.g. calendar months versus 4-4-5 weekly periods).

HR

▮ Establish common naming rules for the roles that exist in the current organisations, as well as those (job titles and departments) that will apply in the future organisation. This may still evolve in the first months after Day One, but ensuring clarity around the actual job content underlining some job titles will save significant time when work begins on the detailed design of the future integrated organisation.

▮ Review by a third party of pension schemes of both companies, comparative analysis of costs and benefits, identification of issues relating to the merger, absorption or alignment of the two pension schemes.

▮ Check integrity of current HR data:

  ◌ Up-dated organisation charts.

  ◌ Detailed listing of all the individuals and jobs involved

in the company, with the headcount broken-down into full-time, part-time, temporary contractor, consultant, vacant position, absent from the organisation (either on maternity leave, long term sickness, hired but not yet commenced in job, notice given and no longer on active duty), resigned but still in the organisation, etc.

○ For each individual identified in the headcount listing: current salary, bonus level, benefits package, statutory or contractual notice period, hierarchical band level.

○ Reconcile the above headcount details with those arising from the organisation charts and those provided by pay-roll, and identify the causes of discrepancies.

○ One of the typical sources of errors is the fact that some individuals may work part of their time in one function or department, and the rest of their time in another, in which case one same individual may account for two or more 'boxes' on an organisation chart. Contractors or temporary staff will generally appear on the organisation chart but not in the payroll data. Part-time employees may appear individually in the organisation chart, or share one role in pairs. As a result, the number expressed as being the 'headcount' of a department or a whole company will depend on whether this is based on payroll, organisation charts, or Full Time Equivalents: this is the reason why the detailed listing mentioned above is essential to be able to correctly assess the impact of the transition between the current state of the two organisations and their future integrated state.

Manufacturing

▌ Establish common naming conventions and costing definitions.

▌ If the agreed product cost definitions differ significantly from those used in either company and cannot be derived directly from their current cost accounting, historical data can be re-stated using the new agreed common definition. Doing this in advance of Day One allows the analysis leading to the design of the future manufacturing footprint to commence early. Transforming an organisation's manufacturing footprint can be a long-drawn out process, but the availability of comparative production costs, based on common definitions, will also be essential to integrate and prioritise the future company's portfolio of products and services, which is key to being able to show 'one face to the customer'.

▌ Agreement on the criteria underlying the design of the manufacturing footprint.

Procurement Function

▌ List of key suppliers including applicable purchasing terms and renewal dates of significant contracts: this information will be needed almost immediately after the legal transaction has taken place, to identify common suppliers, assess the potential for procurement savings and be aware of which contracts need to be re-negotiated as a matter of priority.

Marketing and Commercial

▌ Customer classification: agree on definitions of categories, groupings, classification, and customer hierarchy structure and prepare a detailed customer list with this data for comparison after Day One.

▌ Product/Service portfolio: agree the relevant model of customer behaviour (i.e. how the market perceives the positioning of the products) and map products/services of each company accordingly, country by country if there are regional variations. This will allow item re-positioning and portfolio rationalisation after Day One.

■ Commercial terms:

    ○ Agree on definitions of terms.

    ○ Prepare a list of key customers (using the 80/20 rule) and the commercial terms that apply to them. This is needed to identify significant common customers, detect on Day One any inconsistencies in the terms offered to any particular customer, and prepare plans to rectify the situation to avoid the profitability erosion that would otherwise result from customers 'cherry-picking' the best terms from both former sets of commercial terms.

IT

■ Inventory of current systems and key interfaces.

■ Inventory of licenses/software usage rights.

■ Comparative analysis of functionality and compatibility of the existing hardware and software used in either company (unless part of the software or hardware is deemed to provide a significant strategic or operational competitive advantage, in which case this would fall into the area of restricted information under competition law).

■ If the above analysis can take place, the outline of a convergence plan can be prepared: this will have the advantage of providing an early rough assessment of the complexity of the IT integration and its likely duration.

The choice of IT system can impact the choice of the future business locations: all other things remaining equal, it is often easier to move into the office premises of the team already accustomed to using the chosen IT system than to train all the staff of one location on the use of a new computer system, as they will at that point in time also need to become familiar with new products, procedures and practices. Switching to a new computer system at the same time might result in "change overload", resulting in costly errors, decreased effectiveness and deficiencies in customer service, which can have long lasting adverse consequences for the company.

Lightning Source UK Ltd.
Milton Keynes UK
23 April 2010